What Everyone Needs To Know About THE HOLY SPIRIT

By
Don Stewart

What Everyone
Needs To Know About
THE
HOLY SPIRIT

By
Don Stewart

What Everyone Needs To Know About The Holy Spirit

Published by Dart Press
Box 6486
Orange, California 92613

ISBN   1-877825-09-3

PRINTED IN THE UNITED STATES OF AMERICA BY
GILLILAND PRINTING INC.
215 NORTH SUMMIT
ARKANSAS CITY, KANSAS 67005

All Scripture quotations are from the New King James Version unless otherwise noted.

Contents

Part IV   The Holy Spirit And The Individual

Summary

INTRODUCTION

This present volume, *What Everyone Needs To Know About The Holy Spirit,* is one of a series of works dealing with common questions concerning the Christian faith. The subject under consideration is the Holy Spirit, and—like the other books in this series—is an introductory work on the subject and not meant to be an exhaustive treatise.

Important Subject

The doctrine of the Holy Spirit is one of the most important subjects a believer can study. From Genesis to Revelation, from the creation of the world to the new heavens and new earth, the Holy Spirit is seen at work in our world. The Holy Spirit is mentioned some 90 times in the Old Testament with at least 18 different titles assigned to Him. He is mentioned more than 260 times in the New Testament with 39 different names and titles. Only two of the 27 books of the New Testament, 2 John and 3 John, do not mention the Holy Spirit. Hence, it is important for us to know as much as possible about who the Holy Spirit is and what He does.

Renewal of Interest

There has been a renewal of interest in the subject of the Holy Spirit in the past two decades. Many books have rolled off the presses that deal with the workings of the Spirit. Unfortunately, too many of them have been combative in tone. Because there is disagreement in the church about the modern-day workings of the Spirit, some people have developed an "us versus them" mentality. This is tragic, because the Holy Spirit, who speaks of our Savior Jesus Christ, should be our rallying point, not the issue that divides us.

This books answers questions about the person and work of the Holy Spirit. It will not steer away from controversial questions, but will attempt to answer them in a straightforward way, presenting all sides of the issues.

Identity

In the first section we will deal with questions about the identity of the Holy Spirit. Who is He? Is He a force sent from God or is He more than that? Should the Holy Spirit be treated as a person?

The Work of the Holy Spirit

Once we have established the identity of the Holy Spirit, we will discover what the Bible says about the way He works. How did the Holy Spirit work during the Old Testament period? What happened on the Day of Pentecost? How will the Holy Spirit work in the future?

Spiritual Gifts

Part three observes what the Bible says about spiritual gifts. When Christ ascended into heaven He gave gifts through the Holy Spirit to His followers. What are the gifts? Who has them? How are they to function in the church? Are all the gifts that Christ gave still to be exercised today?

The Holy Spirit and the Individual

The last section will answer questions concerning the Holy Spirit and the way He deals with the individual. Who receives the Holy Spirit? How can a person be filled with the Holy Spirit?

It is the author's wish that this work will help build bridges between those who have been divided over the Holy Spirit. The church of Jesus Christ should be unified, especially regarding the Holy Spirit. The Apostle Paul wrote to the Ephesians,

Endeavoring to keep the unity of the Spirit in the bond of peace. There is one body and one Spirit, just as you were called in one hope of your calling (Ephesians 4:3-4).

Let us strive to keep this unity.

PART 1

THE HOLY SPIRIT:
HIS IDENTITY

WHO IS THE
HOLY SPIRIT?

Before we can answer any questions about the Holy Spirit, we must establish a basic understanding of who He is and what He does. The name "Holy Spirit" comes from two Greek words—*hagion*, meaning "holy," and *pneuma*, meaning "spirit."

The Holy Spirit is known by various names, including the "Spirit of God, the "Spirit of Jesus," the "Spirit of Christ," and the "Spirit of truth." Jesus referred to Him as "another Comforter," and the "Helper."

The Eternal God

The Bible makes it clear that the Holy Spirit is God. We can determine that the Holy Spirit is God in the following ways: He is called God, He is treated on an equal basis with God the Father and God the Son, He has the characteristics of God, and He does the work of God.

Called God by Name

The primary reason we believe the Holy Spirit to be God is because the Scripture clearly affirms this. In the second verse of the Bible He is called the Spirit of God:

The earth was without form, and void; and darkness was on the face of the deep. And the Spirit of God was hovering over the face of the waters (Genesis 1:2).

The Bible designates the Holy Spirit as the Spirit of the Lord God: "The Spirit of the Lord God is upon Me" (Isaiah 61:1).

God of the Old Testament

A close check of Scripture will show that the Holy Spirit is the God of the Old Testament. For example, Isaiah heard the voice of the Lord:

> I hear the voice of the Lord, saying, 'Whom shall I send, and who will go for Us?' Then I said, 'Here am I! Send me' (Isaiah 6:8).

The New Testament identifies the voice that spoke to Isaiah as the voice of the Holy Spirit:

> So when they did not agree among themselves, they departed after Paul had said one word: 'The Holy Spirit spoke rightly through Isaiah the prophet to our fathers' (Acts 28:25).

In the New Testament we find the following account:

> But a certain man named Ananias, with Sapphira his wife, sold a possession. And he kept back part of the proceeds, his wife also being aware of it, and brought a certain part and laid it at the apostles' feet. But Peter said, 'Ananias, why has Satan filled your heart to lie to the Holy Spirit, and to keep back part of the price of the land for yourself . . . You have not lied to men but to God' (Acts 5:1-4).

The Apostle Peter made it clear that Ananias did not lie to man, but to God. The person He lied to is the Holy Spirit. The conclusion is obvious: the Holy Spirit is God.

Equal to the Father and the Son

The Holy Spirit is not only called God; He is also associated on an equal basis with the two other members of the Godhead, the Father and the Son. Jesus said:

> Go therefore and make disciples of all the nations, baptizing them in the name of the Father and of the Son and of the Holy Spirit (Matthew 28:19).

The Apostle Paul wrote:

The grace of our Lord Jesus Christ, and the love of God, and the communion of the Holy Spirit be with you all (2 Corinthians 13:14).

Therefore, the Holy Spirit is linked by association to the other members of the Godhead. This provides further testimony that they are of the same nature, for neither man nor angel is ever associated on the same level with God.

Some biblical attributes of the Holy Spirit belong to God alone:

The Spirit of God is Everywhere Present

Where can I go from Your Spirit? Or where can I flee from Your presence? (Psalm 139:7).

He is All-Knowing

But God has revealed them to us through His Spirit. For the Spirit searches all things, yes, the deep things of God. For what man knows the things of a man except the spirit of man which is in him? Even so no one knows the things of God except the Spirit of God (1 Corinthians 2:10,11).

Who has directed the Spirit of the Lord, or as His counselor taught Him? (Isaiah 40:13).

He is Called the Eternal Spirit

How much more shall the blood of Christ, who through the eternal Spirit offered Himself without spot to God (Hebrews 9:14).

These attributes which the Bible ascribes to the Holy Spirit (all-knowing, everywhere present, and eternal), belong to God and to God alone.

Performs the Work of God

The Holy Spirit performs certain works that only God can perform. For instance, the Bible teaches that He was involved in the creation of the universe:

The earth was without form, and void; and darkness was on the face of the deep. And the Spirit of God was hovering over the face of the waters (Genesis 1:2).

The Holy Spirit was also involved in the creation of life.

The Spirit of God has made me, and the breath of the Almighty give me life (Job 33:4).

Inspired the Bible

The Holy Spirit is the ultimate source behind the books of the Bible.

Knowing this first, that no prophecy of Scripture is of any private interpretation, for prophecy never came by the will of man, but holy men of God spoke as they were moved by the Holy Spirit (2 Peter 1:20,21).

Since all Scripture is God-breathed (2 Timothy 3:16), the Holy Spirit, the source of biblical truth, is God.

Life of Christ

The Holy Spirit is the divine agent that brought Jesus, God the Son, into the world.

And the angel answered and said to her, 'The Holy Spirit will come upon you, and the power of the Highest will overshadow you; therefore, that Holy One who is to be born will be called the Son of God' (Luke 1:35).

The Bible says that it was the Holy Spirit who guided Jesus during His earthly life and was instrumental in His resurrection.

Then Jesus returned in the power of the Spirit to Galilee and news of Him went out through all the surrounding region (Luke 4:14).

And declared to be the Son of God with power according to the Spirit of holiness, by the resurrection from the dead (Romans 1:4).

All of these works are works of God, for no being less than God can perform them.

Titles of His Deity

The Holy Spirit is designated by a number of titles that set forth His deity. They include:

1. The Spirit (John 3:6-8)

2. The Holy Spirit (Luke 11:13)

3. The Spirit of God (1 Corinthians 3:16)

4. The Spirit of the Lord (Isaiah 63:14)

5. The Spirit of the Lord God (Isaiah 61:1)

6. The Spirit of the Living God (2 Corinthians 3:3)

7. The Spirit of the Father (Matthew 10:20)

8. The Spirit of Jesus (Acts 16:6,7)

9. The Holy Spirit of God (Ephesians 4:30)

10. The Spirit of Christ (Romans 8:9)

11. The Spirit of Jesus Christ (Philippians 1:19)

12. The Spirit of His Son (Galatians 4:6)

13. The Spirit which is of God (1 Corinthians 2:12)

These titles set forth the fact that the Holy Spirit is God. They also show, however, that He is a distinct Person from God the Father and God the Son.

Third Person of Trinity

The Holy Spirit is the third person of the Trinity. The doctrine of the Trinity, simply stated, is as follows: The Bible teaches that there is one eternal God who is the Creator and Sustainer of the universe. He is the only God that exists. Within the nature of this one God are three eternal persons, The Father, the Son, and the Holy Spirit. These three persons are the one God. The Trinity doctrine is based on what the Scripture says concerning the nature of God. As we have seen, the Holy Spirit is called God though He is a distinct person from God the Father and God the Son. (For more on what the Bible says about the Trinity, see Don Stewart, *What Everyone Needs To Know About God,* Orange, California, Dart Press, 1992.).

Conclusion

After a close study of Scripture, we can conclude the following:

1. The Holy Spirit is called God.

2. The Holy Spirit is associated on an equal basis with the Father and the Son.

3. The Holy Spirit has the characteristics of God.

4. The Holy Spirit does work only God can do.

We conclude that the Holy Spirit is the eternal God.

IS THE HOLY SPIRIT A PERSON?

The Holy Spirit, to many people, is an enigma. Some see Him as an impersonal force or influence, some deny His very existence, and others are not certain who or what the Holy Spirit is. The Bible, as we have established, teaches that the Holy Spirit is a person, the Third Person of the Holy Trinity. By "person" we mean one who has his own identity or individuality as a rational being, conscious of his own existence. The fact that the Holy Spirit is a person can be observed in four ways: He has the characteristics of a person, He acts like a person, He is treated as a person, and He is the Third Person of the Trinity, and therefore, personal.

Characteristics of a Person

The Scriptures attribute to the Holy Spirit characteristics that only a person can possess. He is portrayed as a thinking being, an emotional being, and a volitional (choosing) being.

A Thinking Being

The Bible says that the Holy Spirit has the intellectual capacity to think:

But God has revealed them to us through His Spirit. For the Spirit searches all things, yes, the deep things of God (1 Corinthians 2:10).

The Holy Spirit thinks and reasons. These things imply personality.

An Emotional Being

The Holy Spirit not only thinks like a person. He has feelings like a person. He can give and receive love.

Now I beg you, brethren, through the Lord Jesus Christ, and through the love of the Spirit, that you strive together with me in your prayers to God for me (Romans 15:30).

He can be grieved:

And do not grieve the Holy Spirit of God, by whom you were sealed for the day of redemption (Ephesians 4:30).

The Holy Spirit can be insulted:

Of how much worse punishment, do you suppose, will he be thought worthy who has trampled the Son of God underfoot, counted the blood of the covenant by which he was sanctified a common thing, and insult the Spirit of grace (Hebrews 10:29).

He responds emotionally the way that a person responds.

A Choosing Being

The Holy Spirit also has a will to choose:

But one and the same Spirit works all these things, distributing to each one individually as He wills (1 Corinthians 12:11).

These attributes are consistent with personhood. Therefore, we see that the characteristics ascribed to the Holy Spirit—thought, feelings, choice—are attributes of a person.

Acts of the Holy Spirit

The deeds that the Holy Spirit performs are deeds only a person can do.

Teaching

These things we also speak not in words which man's wisdom teaches but which the Holy Spirit teaches, comparing spiritual things with spiritual (1 Corinthians 2:13).

Giving Guidance

For as many as are led by the Spirit of God, these are the sons of God (Romans 8:14).

Comforting

Nevertheless I tell you the truth; It is expedient for you that I go away; for if I do not go away, the Comforter will not come to you; but if I depart, I will send him to you (John 16:7 KJV).

Commanding

Then the Spirit said to Philip, 'Go near and overtake this chariot' (Acts 8:29).

Giving Understanding

However, when He, the Spirit of truth, has come, He will guide you into all truth; for He will not speak on His own authority, but whatever He hears He will speak (John 16:13).

Speaking

As they ministered to the Lord and fasted, the Holy Spirit said, 'Now separate to Me Barnabas and Saul for the work which I have called them' (Acts 13:2).

These deeds attributed to the Holy Spirit are not the acts of an impersonal force; they are acts of a person.

Treated as a Person

Whenever the Holy Spirit is encountered in a historical situation we discover that He is always treated as a person. The Bible records that Ananias and Sapphira lied to the Holy Spirit.

But Peter said, 'Ananias, why has Satan filled your heart to lie to the Holy Spirit and keep back part of the price of the land for yourself ' (Acts 5:3).

You can lie only to a person.
Stephen told the Sanhedrin that they were disobeying the Holy Spirit by resisting Him:

You stiff-necked and uncircumcised in heart and ears! You always resist the Holy Spirit; as your fathers did, so do you (Acts 7:51).

You do not disobey an impersonal force, you disobey a person.
On another occasion Simon Peter went to the house of Cornelius as the Holy Spirit directed:

While Peter thought about the vision, the Spirit said to him, 'Behold three men are seeking you' (Acts 10:19).

Consequently whenever we find the Holy Spirit in a historical narrative He is consistently treated as though He is a person, never as anything less.

Part of the Godhead

The final reason that we conclude that the Holy Spirit is a person is that He is addressed as God. He is a member of the Godhead which consists of the Father, Son, and Holy Spirit. Jesus said:

Go therefore and make disciples of all the nations, baptizing them in the name of the Father and of the Son and of the Holy Spirit (Matthew 28:19).

The Father and Son are personal beings and the Holy Spirit is treated in the same manner and assumed to be a person.

Blasphemed

Jesus taught that the Holy Spirit could be blasphemed:

Therefore I say to you, every sin and blasphemy against the Spirit will not be forgiven men (Matthew 12:31).

Only God can be blasphemed. Thus, if the Holy Spirit is God and God is personal, then the Holy Spirit must be personal.

Why Neuter Gender?

As mentioned before, the Greek word translated "spirit" is *pneuma* which means "wind," "breath." or "spirit," Like many languages, Greek attaches gender-masculine, feminine, or neuter—to each noun. The word *pneuma* is neuter. Does this mean the Holy Spirit is impersonal? Not at all. This is because grammatical gender is not the same as personal gender. The fact that a word is spoken in the neuter has nothing to do with its personal gender.

Also some have argued that the New Testament breaks the normal rules of grammar to show that the Holy Spirit is a person. We find masculine personal pronouns used in reference to the Holy Spirit. This contradicts the normal rules of grammar. Usually the pronoun agrees with the word is substituted for in the same grammatical gender. However, when referring to the Holy Spirit, the Scripture substitutes a masculine pronoun. Jesus used the masculine demonstrative pronoun when referring to the Holy Spirit:

However, when He, the Spirit of truth, has come, He will guide you into all truth; for He will not speak on His own authority, but whatever He hears He will speak; and He will tell you things to come. He will glorify Me, for He will take of what is Mine, and declare it to you (John 16:13,14).

Consequently, the neuter gender does not at all signify that the Holy Spirit is some impersonal force. He is indeed the personal Spirit of God.

Why Considered Impersonal?

There have been those who cite Scripture to prove the Holy Spirit is an impersonal force or influence. Several reasons are given for this belief.

Like the Wind

The Holy Spirit is spoken of as being the "Spirit of God." The word translated Spirit can also be translated "breath" or "wind" which implies an unseen impersonal force. Yet the Scripture uses the symbol of the wind to describe the invisible way in which the Holy Spirit acts not to imply that He is some impersonal influence.

Symbols

The Holy Spirit is symbolized by impersonal objects such as wind, water, fire, and oil. Some conclude that this means the Holy Spirit Himself is impersonal. Yet the Scripture also gives many symbols for God the Father and God the Son. Jesus, for example, is symbolized as a rock and a door. This, however, does not mean He is some force or influence. Likewise the symbols used of the Holy Spirit do not negate His personality.

Invisible

The work of the Holy Spirit is invisible. This to some implies a non-personal entity. The fact, however, that the Holy Spirit is invisible does not mean He is less than a person. According to Jesus, God the Father is also invisible. He said "God is Spirit" (John 4:24).

It is true that we have a harder time relating to the personality of the Holy Spirit than to God the Father and God the Son. The titles "Father" and "Son" generate feelings of personality to us while the title "Holy Spirit" is a bit harder to relate. Nevertheless the Scripture clearly teaches that the Holy Spirit is a person despite the fact that He is invisible and has not corporeal form.

Conclusion

We conclude the following concerning the Holy Spirit:

1. The Holy Spirit has the attributes of a person.

2. The Spirit also performs the acts of a person.

3. The Holy Spirit is treated as a person.

4. The Holy Spirit is God, and therefore, by nature is personal.

5. All attempts to make the Holy Spirit an impersonal force or influence does not take in all the evidence. It is clear from Scripture that the Holy Spirit is a person.

SHOULD THE HOLY SPIRIT BE SINGLED OUT FOR WORSHIP?

Since the Holy Spirit is God, should He be singled out for worship? The Bible says that the Holy Spirit's job is not glorify Himself but rather to glorify Christ. Jesus made this clear:

> But when the Helper comes, whom I shall send to you from the Father, the Spirit of truth who proceeds from the Father, He will testify of Me (John 15:26).

> However, when He, the Spirit of truth, has come, He will guide you into all truth; for He will not speak on His own authority, but whatever He hears He will speak; and He will tell you things to come. He will glorify Me, for He will take care of Mine and declare it to you (John 16:13,14).

Thus, the Holy Spirit should not be singled out for worship.

No Worship?

Does this mean we should not worship the Holy Spirit at all? Though some would say we should not, the fact is that we *do* worship the Holy Spirit. To deny worship to the Holy Spirit is to deny His deity. According to the dictionary, worship is "the reverent love accorded to a deity, idol, or sacred object . . . to honor or love as deity." The famous preacher R. A. Torrey wrote:

Worship is a definite act of the creature in relation to God. Worship is bowing to God in adoring acknowledgment and contemplation of Himself and the perfection of His being (R. A. Torrey, *The Person and Work of the Holy Spirit*, Zondervan, p. 133).

Shouldn't the Holy Spirit, therefore, be accorded worship? The historic church thought so and even preserved prayers to the Holy Spirit from the fourth century until today. The Eastern Orthodox, Roman Catholic, and most mainline Protestant denominations still use hymns and prayers to the Holy Spirit.

One possible translation of Philippians 3:3 says that we do worship the Holy Spirit. "For we are the circumcision, who worship the Spirit of God." Though there may be no direct commandments to single out the Holy Spirit for worship, we do worship Him when we worship God because the Holy Spirit is God.

WHO ARE THE SEVEN SPIRITS?

A number of times in the Book of Revelation there is a reference to the "seven Spirits."

> John, to the seven churches which are in Asia: Grace to you and peace from Him who is and who was and who is to come, and from the seven Spirits who are before His throne (Revelation 1:4).

> And to the angel of the church of Sardis write, 'These things says He who has the seven Spirits of God and the seven stars' (Revelation 3:1).

References to the seven Spirits are also made in Revelation 4:5 and 5:6. Who are these "Spirits"?

One Holy Spirit

Again, we emphasize that the Bible teaches there is only one Holy Spirit:

> But one and the same Spirit works all these things, distributing to each one individually as He wills (1 Corinthians 12:11).

To this verse many others could be added. The united testimony of Scripture is that there is only one Spirit of God.

Consequently, this expression "seven Spirits" does not refer to seven different spirits. It could refer to the different ways the Spirit of God expresses Himself. Some see an explanation of the seven Spirits in the Book of Isaiah:

The Spirit of the Lord shall rest upon Him, the spirit of wisdom and understanding, the spirit of counsel and might, the spirit of knowledge and the fear of the Lord (Isaiah 11:2).

Therefore, the "seven Spirits" are not different spirits but most likely refer to the complex ministry of the one Holy Spirit.

IS THERE A COUNTERFEIT
HOLY SPIRIT?

The Bible speaks of not only the genuine Spirit of God but also of a counterfeit. Paul warned the church at Corinth:

> But I fear, lest somehow, as the serpent deceived Eve by his craftiness, so your minds may be corrupted from the simplicity that is in Christ. For if he who comes preaches another Jesus whom we have not preached, or if you receive a different spirit which you have not received, or a different gospel which you have not accepted, you may well put up with it. . . For such are false apostles, deceitful workers, transforming themselves into apostles of Christ. And no wonder! For Satan himself transforms himself into an angel of light (2 Corinthians 11:3,4, 13,14).

Test the Spirits

We are warned about a counterfeit Holy Spirit. A thing that is counterfeit always is made to look as close as possible to the genuine article. This lets us know that everything that claims to proceed from the Holy Spirit is not necessarily from the Holy Spirit. We must test the spirits.

> Beloved, do not believe every spirit, but test the spirits, whether they are of God; because many false prophets are gone out into the world (1 John 4:1).

WHAT SYMBOLS DOES THE BIBLE USE TO DESCRIBE THE HOLY SPIRIT?

The Bible uses a number of symbols to describe the person and work of the Holy Spirit. They symbols show the nature, character and work of the Holy Spirit. They include:

Water

The Holy Spirit is symbolized by water which speaks of refreshing, cleansing and washing the believer of his sins. Jesus said:

> 'If anyone thirsts, let him come to Me and drink. He who believes in Me, as the Scripture has said, out of his heart will flow rivers of living water.' But this He spoke of the Spirit, whom those believing in Him would receive; for the Holy Spirit was not yet given, because Jesus was not yet glorified (John 7:37-39).

Wind or Breath

The wind symbolizes the invisible yet powerful work of the Holy Spirit.

> And suddenly there came a sound from heaven, as of a rushing mighty wind, and it filled the whole house where they were sitting (Acts 2:2).

Fire

Fire speaks of the holiness of God and the judging of sin in the life of the believer.

> When the Lord has washed away the filth of the daughters of Zion, and purged the blood of Jerusalem from her midst, by the spirit of judgment and by the spirit of burning (Isaiah 4:4).

Oil

Oil was involved in the anointing of the prophets, priests and kings for ministry to their offices. Oil symbolizes the soothing and healing presence of the Holy Spirit.

> God anointed Jesus of Nazareth with the Holy Spirit and with power, who went about doing good and healing all who were oppressed by the devil, for God was with Him (Acts 10:38).

Dove

The dove represents the gentleness and peace which the Holy Spirit provides the believer.

> And the Holy Spirit descended in bodily form like a dove upon Him, and a voice came from heaven which said, 'You are My beloved Son; in You I am well pleased' (Luke 3:22).

Still Small Voice

The Spirit is the voice of God that speaks to our innermost being.

> Then He said, 'Go out and stand on the mountain of the Lord.' And behold, the Lord passed by, and a great and strong wind tore into the mountains and broke the rocks in pieces before the Lord, but the Lord was not in the wind; and after the wind an earthquake, but the Lord was not in the earthquake; and after the earthquake a fire, but the Lord was not in the fire; and after the fire a still small voice. So it was, when Elijah heard it, that he wrapped his face in his mantle and went out and stood in the entrance of the cave. And suddenly a voice came to him, and said, 'What are you doing here, Elijah?' (1 Kings 19:11-13).

Firstfruits

The firstfruits were a symbol of the coming harvest. The initial work of the Holy Spirit symbolizes the final salvation and glorification of each believer.

And not only they, but we also who have the firstfruits of the Spirit, even we ourselves groan within ourselves, eagerly waiting for the adoption, the redemption of our body (Romans 8:23).

Earnest

The earnest was the downpayment, a pledge of more to come. The Spirit pledges that our salvation will be completed when we are glorified with Christ.

Who has sealed us and given us the Spirit as a deposit (2 Corinthians 1:11).

Enduement

Enduement speaks of the divine clothing of the believer with the Holy Spirit. Jesus said to His disciples:

Behold, I send the Promise of My Father upon you; but tarry in the city of Jerusalem until you are endued with power from on high (Luke 24:49).

Number Seven

Seven speaks of completion. When used of the Holy Spirit it symbolizes the Spirit's fulness and perfection.

John, to the seven churches which are in Asia: Grace to you and peace from Him who is and who was and who is to come, and from the seven Spirits who are before His throne (Revelation 1:4).

These different symbols that the Bible uses to describe the person and work of the Holy Spirit will begin to give us an idea of how He works in our life.

Holy Spirit or Holy Ghost?

When we read the Bible in the King James Version we find the Spirit of God variously referred to as the "Holy Spirit" and the "Holy Ghost." Is there a reason that these two different designations are used? Is it speaking of two different personalities or is it referring to two different aspects of the one Spirit?

Actually, these verses refer to the one Holy Spirit. There is no theological reason why the Holy Spirit is sometimes referred to as the Holy Ghost. The reason for the difference if found in the story behind the translation of the King James Bible. When the King James Version was translated it was done by different committees. One of the committees consistently translated the Greek words *hagion pneuma* as "Holy Spirit" while the other committee translated it as "Holy Ghost." When the translation was completed these differences remained. Thus, you have the Spirit of God referred to as both the Holy Spirit and the Holy Ghost.

Modern translations have corrected this inconsistency and have uniformly translated the phrase *hagion pneuma* as Holy Spirit.

CONCLUSION TO PART 1

Having investigated what the Bible says about the nature or identity of the Holy Spirit, we can conclude the following:

1. The Holy Spirit is the eternal God, the Third Person of the Trinity. He is known by different designations including the Holy Ghost, the Spirit of Christ, the Spirit of Jesus, the Helper, and the Comforter.

2. The Holy Spirit, as the eternal God, deserves our worship.

3. Though He is called different names there is only one Holy Spirit.

4. The Holy Spirit is personal. He is not an impersonal force or influence.

5. The Bible describes the Holy Spirit with many symbols which signify His work among us.

PART 2

THE HOLY SPIRIT:
HIS WORKS

HOW DOES THE HOLY SPIRIT WORK?

The Holy Spirit works in ways beyond our understanding. Jesus compared the Spirit to the wind:

> The wind blows where it wishes, and you hear the sound of it, but cannot tell where it comes from and where it goes. So is everyone who is born of the Spirit (John 3:8).

This reveals several things about the work of the Holy Spirit.

As He Desires

The Holy Spirit works in a sovereign manner. He works in the way He desires. The work of the Spirit is in accordance to the purposes of God. As the wind blows where it wishes, so the Spirit of God works where He desires.

Invisible

Like the wind, the work of the Holy Spirit cannot be seen with our eyes. We see the results of the wind but not the wind itself. The same holds true for the work of the Spirit. The Spirit's work in a person's life is invisible to everyone. Yet the results of that work—a changed life—can, like the results of the wind, be observed.

Powerful

We have all seen the wind whip up in a powerful manner. The Spirit also works in a powerful manner when He touches someone's life.

On the Day of Pentecost, when the Holy Spirit came down upon believers, He did so accompanied by the sound of a mighty rushing wind.

And suddenly there came a sound from heaven, as of a rushing mighty wind, and it filled the whole house where they were sitting (Acts 2:2).

Consequently, we cannot limit His ministry. As the wind is invisible, powerful, and blows where it wishes, so also is the work of the Holy Spirit. Therefore, we must always be careful not to try to make Him conform to the way *we* believe He will work.

HOW DOES THE HOLY SPIRIT HELP RUN THE UNIVERSE?

The Bible teaches that the Holy Spirit is directly involved with the functioning of the universe. The Scripture teaches that the development of the universe from its beginning until the present time has been a work of the Holy Spirit.

Creation

The Holy Spirit help in the original creation.

The earth was without form, and void; and darkness was on the face of the deep. And the Spirit of God was hovering over the face of the waters (Genesis 1:2).

Keeps Universe Running

The orderly running of the universe is another ministry of the Holy Spirit:

Who has measured the waters in the hollow of His hand, measured heaven with a span and calculated the dust of the earth in a measure? Weighed the mountains in scales and the hills in a balance? Who has directed the Spirit of the Lord, or as His counselor has taught Him (Isaiah 40:12,13).

Adorns the Universe

The Holy Spirit adorns the universe with its beauty: "By His Spirit He adorned the heavens (Job 26:13).

Renews the Universe

The preservation and renewal of God's creation is another ministry of the Holy Spirit:

You send forth your Spirit, they are created; and You renew the face of the earth (Psalm 104:30).

Thus the Holy Spirit helped in the creation of the universe, He is involved in the orderly running of the universe, He helped adorn the universe, and He also renews and preserves it. Since these are all works of God, they are further indications that the Holy Spirit is the eternal God.

HOW DID THE HOLY SPIRIT WORK DURING THE OLD TESTAMENT PERIOD?

There are no direct statements in the Old Testament about the relationship of the Holy Spirit to the believer. Thus it is difficult to arrive at any conclusion about the work of the Holy Spirit during the Old Testament period.

There are those who believe the Holy Spirit did not work in the same manner during the Old Testament age as He does today. Although it has been the same Holy Spirit all along, His methods have changed from age to age. They contend that the indwelling of the Holy Spirit in the Old Testament was not universal to every believer, but was available only to certain believers.

No Promise of Indwelling

There is no promise in the Old Testament to the believer that he will be indwelt with the Holy Spirit.

And the Lord said to Moses: 'Take Joshua the son of Nun with you, a man in whom is the Spirit, lay your hand on him' (Numbers 27:18).

This verse seems to indicate that the Holy Spirit is not to be found in everyone. By stating that the Holy Spirit is in Joshua, it infers He is not universally given. The Spirit is said to have come upon other individuals, such as Othniel:

The Spirit of the Lord came upon him and he judged
Israel (Judges 3:10).

The reason this view—that only certain individuals
were indwelt with the Holy Spirit—is held is based upon an
understanding of a statement made by Jesus:

> Even the Spirit of truth, whom the world cannot
> receive, because it neither sees Him nor knows Him; but
> you know Him, for He dwells with you and will be in you
> (John 14:17).

This verse is interpreted to mean that the Holy Spirit
was only with believers during Old Testament times but
now dwells within each believer in the New Testament age.
Not only was the Spirit limited to certain individuals;
the extent of the indwelling was limited. He could leave an
individual after He had indwelt them. The life of Saul serves
as an example:

> When they came to there to the hill, there was a group
> of prophets to meet him; then the Spirit of God came
> upon him and he prophesied among them (1 Samuel
> 10:10).

> But the Spirit of the Lord departed from Saul, a
> distressing Spirit from the Lord troubled him (1 Samuel
> 16:14).

Yet there is a another way to understand this difficult
passage and the Old Testament references to the Holy
Spirit. It is possible that the references to the Holy Spirit
being upon Joshua and others refer to a "special
anointing" and not the indwelling of the Holy Spirit. The
reason for holding this view is because it is difficult to see
how anyone could have entered a right relationship with
God without the Holy Spirit indwelling them. The Bible
teaches that we all have a sinful nature and need to be
saved from our sins. If the Holy Spirit did not indwell
individuals during the Old Testament period, how were
they saved and how did they lead a godly life? It seems
impossible for them to be able to do so without the
indwelling of the Holy Spirit. Jesus told Nicodemus:

> Unless one is born of water and the Spirit, he cannot
> enter the kingdom of God (John 3:5, KJV).

According to Jesus, everyone has to have a spiritual rebirth to enter God's kingdom. Furthermore, no one can serve God in his own strength. It seems more consistent to say that the Holy Spirit indwelt everyone who believed in the promises of God.

Special Ability

The Old Testament records the Holy Spirit giving special ability to certain individuals:

> Then the Lord spoke to Moses, saying: 'See, I have called by name Bezaleel the son of Uri, the son of Hur, of the tribe of Judah. And I have filled him with the Spirit of God, in wisdom, in understanding, in knowledge, and in all manner of workmanship' (Exodus 31:1-3).

The Holy Spirit's ministry to the world has existed from the beginning of time as a restraining influence. This is as true today as it was during the Old Testament period. The Holy Spirit's influence kept sin from running entirely rampant.

We may conclude that the Old Testament teaches the following regarding the Holy Spirit:

1. The Bible does not give a comprehensive picture about the work of the Holy Spirit during the Old Testament period.

2. Some people believe the Bible teaches that the Holy Spirit could leave those whom He did indwell.

3. It seems more plausible that the leaving of the Holy Spirit's was the leaving of the Spirit's anointing rather than His indwelling.

4. During the Old Testament period the Holy Spirit gave some believers special skills to perform certain tasks.

5. With regard to the unbelieving world, the Holy Spirit acted as a restraining influence.

WHAT WAS THE RELATIONSHIP OF THE HOLY SPIRIT TO THE EARTHLY LIFE OF JESUS?

The Holy Spirit is not only related to Jesus in His deity, as a member of the Trinity. He is also related to Jesus in His humanity.

Birth

The Scriptures teach that the Holy Spirit was involved in the conception of Jesus.

And the angel answered (Mary) and said to her, 'The Holy Spirit will come upon you, and the power of the Highest will overshadow you; therefore, also, that Holy One who is to be born will be called the Son of God' (Luke 1:35).

The Holy Spirit, through the Virgin Mary, conceived the child Jesus.

Baptism

The Holy Spirit was also involved in Jesus' baptism. When John baptized Him, the Holy Spirit descended in a bodily form, identifying Jesus as the Messiah.

And the Holy Spirit descended in bodily form like a
dove upon Him, and a voice came from heaven which said,
'You are My beloved Son; in You I am well pleased' (Luke
4:22).

Temptation

Luke records that Jesus was led by the Holy Spirit into
the wilderness to be tempted by the devil.

Then Jesus, being filled with the Holy Spirit, returned
from the Jordan and was led by the Spirit into the
wilderness (Luke 4:1).

Public Ministry

The public ministry of Jesus was performed through
the power of the Holy Spirit. "Then Jesus returned in the
power of the Spirit to Galilee, and the news of Him went out
through all the surrounding region" (Luke 4:14). Jesus
Himself testified that the Spirit of the Lord was upon Him.

The Spirit of the Lord is upon Me, because He has
anointed Me to preach the gospel to the poor. He has sent
Me to heal the brokenhearted, to preach deliverance to
the captives and recovery of sight to the blind, to set at
liberty those who are oppressed . . . Today this Scripture
is fulfilled in your ears (Luke 4:18,21).

Miracles

During His public ministry, Jesus performed miracles
by the power of the Holy Spirit.

But, if I cast out demons by the Spirit of God, surely
the kingdom of God has come upon you (Matthew 12:28).

The signs He performed were done in obedience to the
Father through the agency of the Holy Spirit.

The Resurrection

The Holy Spirit was also at work in the resurrection of
Christ.

But if the Spirit of Him who raised Jesus from the
dead, He who raised Christ will also give life to your

mortal bodies through His Spirit who dwells in you
(Romans 8:11).

The Spirit of God brought Jesus back from the dead.
Therefore, as we study Scripture we find the Holy Spirit
played a vital role in the life and ministry of Jesus being
involved with Him from His conception through His
resurrection.

WHAT IS THE BLASPHEMY OF THE HOLY SPIRIT?

Jesus spoke of a sin called the blasphemy of the Holy Spirit. What is it? Can someone who commits this sin be forgiven?

The background of Jesus' statement can be found in Matthew 12:22-30. Jesus healed a man who was possessed by a demon. His demon possession made him blind, mute, and probably deaf. This combination of illnesses made it impossible for anyone to cast the demon out of the man because there was no way anyone could communicate with him. When the people saw Jesus heal the man, they wondered if He could be the Messiah.

The suggestion that Jesus could be the Messiah brought a quick response from the religious leaders. "But when the Pharisees heard it they said, 'This fellow does not cast out demons except by Beelzebub, the ruler of the demons' " (Matthew 12:24).

They accused Jesus of casting out demons by the power of Satan. Who would want to follow someone who is working with Satan?

Jesus responded by showing how illogical their arguments were (Matthew 12:25-30). He then made this statement:

Therefore I say to you, every sin and blasphemy will be forgiven men, but the blasphemy against the Spirit will not be forgiven men. Anyone who speaks a word against the Son of Man, it will be forgiven him; but whoever speaks against the Holy Spirit, it will not be forgiven him, either in this age or in the age to come (Matthew 12:31,32).

From the statements of Jesus we learn the following concerning the blasphemy of the Holy Spirit:

1. The sin was against the Holy Spirit. The accusation made by the Pharisees was not only against Christ; ultimately it was against the Holy Spirit who was performing the miracles through Christ.

2. Those who sin against Jesus can be forgiven. But sinning against the Holy Spirit, who personifies the power of God, is unforgivable. There could be no question that the miracle had been through the power of the Holy Spirit. Those who attribute the Holy Spirit's work to Satan cannot expect to be forgiven.

3. The blasphemy of the Holy Spirit is more than one particular sin; it is a continuous state of being. The religious leaders were constantly attributing the works of Christ, through the Holy Spirit, to the devil. This revealed the evil condition of their hearts.

4. The consequences of blaspheming the Holy Spirit meant eternal damnation. There could be no forgiveness in this life or in eternity.

HOW DOES SOMEONE TODAY BLASPHEME THE HOLY SPIRIT?

When Christ was on earth the Holy Spirit was blasphemed when His works were attributed to the devil. How does one blaspheme the Holy Spirit today?

We must first understand that His situation was unique. Christ was physically present, performing miracles through the Holy Spirit's power to testify that He was the Messiah. But He is not with us today in a physical presence. How then does blasphemy of the Holy Spirit occur.

The work of the Holy Spirit is still the same: to speak of Jesus Christ and to show the world it needs His forgiveness:

> Nevertheless I tell you the truth. It is to your advantage that I go away; for if I do not go away, the Helper will not come to you; but if I depart, I will send Him to you. And when He has come, He will convict the world of sin, and of righteousness, and of judgment: of sin, because they do not believe in Me; of righteousness, because I go to My Father and you see Me no more; of judgment, because the ruler of this world is judged (John 16:7-11).

Therefore, the blasphemy of the Holy Spirit is unbelief. Those who continually reject the Holy Spirit's work portraying Christ as Savior as blaspheming the Holy Spirit. If this state continues they will not receive forgiveness for their sins.

Thus, today, as in Christ's time, the blasphemy of the Holy Spirit is a continuous state of being rather than one particular sin. It is the state of unbelief.

We conclude regarding the blasphemy of the Holy Spirit:

1. People today are not in the same situation as when Christ was physically present.

2. Today one blasphemes the Holy Spirit by rejecting the ministry of the Holy Spirit that speaks of Christ.

3. Thus the blasphemy of the Holy Spirit is the state of unbelief in Christ as Savior. It is more of a continuing and persistent rejection of the Holy Spirit than one particular sin.

4. The only way to avoid the blasphemy of the Holy Spirit is to turn to Christ for forgiveness.

WHAT HAPPENED ON THE DAY OF PENTECOST?

One of the most significant events recorded in the Bible happened on the Day of Pentecost. The Holy Spirit came down to permanently indwell the disciples, and the church age began.

The New Testament gives the description of the events:

Now when the Day of Pentecost had fully come, they were all with one accord in one place. And suddenly there came a sound from heaven, as of a rushing, mighty wind, and it filled the whole house where they were sitting. Then there appeared to them divided tongues, as of fire, and one sat on each of them. And they were all filled with the Holy Spirit and began to speak with other tongues, as the Spirit gave them utterance (Acts 2:1-4).

Several significant things happened on the Day of Pentecost. They include:

Fulfillment of Prophecy

On the Day of Pentecost prophecy was fulfilled. Acts 2:1 literally reads, "As the Day of Pentecost was being fulfilled." What was fulfilled was the prophecy given by both Jesus and John the Baptist concerning the coming of the Holy Spirit. John had earlier said of Jesus:

> I indeed baptize you with water unto repentance, but He who is coming after Me is mightier than I . . . He will baptize you with the Holy Spirit and fire (Matthew 3:11).

Ten days before Pentecost Jesus reiterated the prediction. "

> For John truly baptized with water, but you shall be baptized with the Holy Spirit not many days from now (Acts 1:5).

The coming of the Holy Spirit also was to give power to the believers:

> But you shall receive power when the Holy Spirit has come upon you; and you shall be witnesses to Me in Jerusalem, and in all Judea and Samaria, and to the end of the earth (Acts 1:8).

When Pentecost occurred, the Holy Spirit came as promised, baptizing the believers into Christ and giving them power to be His witnesses.

Beginning of the Church Age

Pentecost was also the birthday of the church. The Old Testament period of law was concluded and a new era began. Those who believe in Jesus as Messiah during this present age become part of the body (or bride) of Christ known as the church. The church age began at Pentecost and will conclude when Christ comes back for His own.

Signs Following

The Day of Pentecost also witnessed signs which followed the coming of the Holy Spirit. As Jesus had predicted those who believed spoke with new tongues:

> And these signs shall follow those who believe: In My name they will cast out demons; they will speak with new tongues (Mark 16:17).

These tongues were unknown languages that the disciples were supernaturally enabled to speak.

First Converts

The Day of Pentecost also saw the first converts to the Christian church. When Simon Peter delivered his sermon proclaiming that Christ had risen, some three thousand people became converted.

Then those who gladly received his word were baptized; and that day about three thousand souls were added to them (Acts 2:41).

Conclusion

We can conclude that on the Day of Pentecost the following occurred: The Holy Spirit, in fulfilling prophecies of both Jesus and John the Baptist, descended in a unique way upon all the believers, giving them power for service; the outpouring of the Holy Spirit began the church age; the disciples were both baptized and filled with the Holy Spirit; the sign of speaking in unknown languages was given to the disciples as evidence of the arrival of the Holy Spirit; and finally, on this birthday of the church when the Holy Spirit descended upon all the believers, Peter preached the first sermon of the church age and three thousand people were converted.

WHAT IS THE BAPTISM OF
THE HOLY SPIRIT?

One of the Holy Spirit's ministries that has attracted much attention is the baptism of the Holy Spirit. What is the baptism of the Holy Spirit? When does it occur? Who receives it?

The phrase "baptism of the Holy Spirit" is not found in the Bible. The Bible speaks of a baptism "with," "by," or "in" the Holy Spirit. It never refers to the baptism "of" the Holy Spirit.

The phrase "baptism with, in, or by the Spirit" occurs seven times in the New Testament (Matthew 3:11; Mark 1:8; Luke 3:16; John 1:33; Acts 1:5;11:16; 1 Corinthians 12:13). This is not the same as water baptism.

Began at Pentecost

The first time people were baptized with the Holy Spirit was on the Day of Pentecost. John the Baptist predicted that Jesus would baptize believers with the Holy Spirit:

> I indeed baptize you with water unto repentance, but He who is coming after Me is mightier than I . . . He will baptize you with the Holy Spirit (Matthew 3:11).

After His death and resurrection, Jesus spoke of the baptism with the Holy Spirit as something still future. At His ascension Jesus told His disciples:

For John truly baptized with water, but you shall be baptized with the Holy Spirit not many days from now (Acts 1:5).

A few years later Simon Peter considered the baptism with the Holy Spirit as something that had already occurred.

And as I began to speak, the Holy Spirit fell upon them, as upon us at the beginning. Then I remembered the word of the Lord, how He said, 'John indeed baptized with water, but you shall be baptized with the Holy Spirit' (Acts 11:15,16).

This reference is obviously to the Day of Pentecost, when the Holy Spirit fell upon the assembled believers. The Holy Spirit came upon believers at a divine time in a designated place.

Baptized into the Body of Christ

The Apostle Paul taught that the baptism with the Holy Spirit is that ministry which places the believer into the body of Christ.

For by one Spirit we were all baptized into one body—whether Jews or Greeks, whether slaves or free—and have been made to drink into one Spirit (1 Corinthians 12:13).

Thus, when one is baptized in the Holy Spirit, it joins him to the body of Christ.

All Believers

The Apostle Paul said the same thing to the church at Galatia.

For as many of you as were baptized into Christ have put on Christ (Galatians 3:27).

Therefore, the baptism with the Holy Spirit is something that all believers have received. Since all believers are said to have been baptized by the Holy Spirit, it must happen at the moment of salvation.

Nonexperiential

The baptism with the Holy Spirit is a non-experiential work of the Spirit. There is no feeling or emotion connected with receiving the baptism with the Holy Spirit. It is a work of God on the believer's behalf that he does not directly experience.

We conclude the following concerning the baptism of the Holy Spirit:

1. Though this particular ministry is popularly referred to as the baptism of the Holy Spirit, the Bible nowhere calls it such. The ministry is more properly spoken of as the baptism "with," "in," or "by" the Holy Spirit.

2. The baptism with the Holy Spirit first occurred at the Day of Pentecost.

3. It is the ministry of the Holy Spirit that places the believer into the body of Christ at the moment of salvation.

4. All believers have been baptized with the Holy Spirit.

5. It is a nonexperiential work of God done on behalf of the believer. Thus one should not expect to experience some emotion or feeling when he is baptized with the Holy Spirit.

IS THE BAPTISM WITH THE HOLY SPIRIT A SECOND EXPERIENCE FOLLOWING SALVATION?

There are some people who contend that each believer needs a second experience subsequent to salvation to give him power. Many refer to this experience as the "baptism with the Holy Spirit." As we have seen, the baptism with the Holy Spirit is a non-experiential work that happens to the believer when he trusts Christ.

The Bible also teaches that there is no need for a second blessing or "crisis" experience for the believer. This is because every spiritual blessing has been given us by God through Jesus Christ. Scripture never commands believers to seek a "second blessing" after salvation. The Apostle Paul told the Ephesians:

Blessed be the God and Father of our Lord Jesus Christ, who has blessed us with every spiritual blessing in the heavenly places in Christ (Ephesians 1:3).

God has also made us complete in Christ:

For in Him dwells all the fullness of the Godhead bodily; and you are complete in Him, who is the head of all principality and power (Colossians 2:9,10).

But we should not take this to mean that the believer should not desire to appropriate the fulness of God's Spirit in their lives. Though all blessings have been given to each believer, he has the privilege and responsibility of applying them to his life. Jesus spoke of the power of the Holy Spirit:

> He who believes in Me, as the Scripture has said, out of his heart will flow rivers of living water. But this He spoke concerning the Spirit whom those believing in Him would receive; for the Holy Spirit was not yet given, because Jesus was not yet glorified (John 7:37-39).

Two Baptisms?

Some people who believe the baptism with the Holy Spirit is a second experience following salvation actually see Scripture speaking of two separate baptisms. They believe that 1 Corinthians 12:13 speaks of the baptism "by" the Spirit that puts believers into the body of Christ. The Book of Acts, they contend, speaks of the baptism "by Christ" to place people "in" the sphere of the Holy Spirit. They believe the first baptism happens at conversion and is experienced by all believers. The second happens after conversion and provides power to the believer. This view teaches that all believers have been baptized *by* the Spirit while not all believers have been baptized *in* the Spirit.

What the Bible Says

It is generally agreed that the references in the gospels look forward to the baptism with the Holy Spirit occurring at the Day of Pentecost. The references in Acts point back to the fulfillment. This being the case, the reference in 1 Corinthians 12:13 seemingly gives the doctrinal explanation of what occurred.

Though it is possible to see two separate baptisms, it seems better to understand all the references explaining the same experience. Charles Ryrie makes an appropriate comment on the subject:

> Such an infrequently used and seemingly technical phrase would more likely refer to the same activity in all its occurrences. To establish two separate and quite distinct baptisms is tenuous at best. To see two agents is biblical because of Acts 2:33 and quite normal because different Persons of the Trinity are involved in the same work. Besides, Ephesians 4:5 says there is only one baptism. It is Christ's work through the agency of the Spirit's ministry to join those who believe to the church, the body of Christ, with all the privileges and responsibilities that come with that position (Charles

Ryrie, *Basic Theology*, Wheaton, Ill., Victor Books, 1986, p. 365).

We can conclude the following:

1. The baptism with the Holy Spirit occurs the moment a person is saved. It is not the same experience as salvation but happens at the time of salvation. It is not a second experience following conversion.

2. God has given believers everything "in Christ." When we are saved we are complete in Him. We lack nothing. There is nothing else for Him to give to us.

3. Nowhere are believers commanded to receive any second blessing that would give them power. All power is already available.

4. The power of the Holy Spirit working in a persons life is something that should be desired, but it is not something that needs to be received separately from salvation. Unfortunately, some who have legitimately experienced the Spirit's power mislabel the experience as the "baptism with the Holy Spirit" whereas the Scripture calls this experience the filling of the Holy Spirit. As previously mentioned, everything has been provided for us upon conversion. We only need to appropriate what God has already done for us. (We will consider this issue further in the next few questions).

DOES THE BAPTISM WITH THE HOLY SPIRIT GUARANTEE THE BELIEVER POWER?

When one is baptized with the Holy Spirit, does He receive special power in His life? Is it something that gives Him added strength to live the victorious Christian life?

As noted previously, the baptizing work of the Holy Spirit places the believer into the body of Christ. This enables Him to receive power but does not guarantee Him any special strength. The believers in the Galatian and Corinthian churches were all baptized by the Holy Spirit, but their lives were far from being spiritually mature.

The Apostle Paul assured the Galatians that they had been baptized in the Holy Spirit.

> For as many of you as were baptized into Christ have put on Christ (Galatians 3:27).

Yet, these same Galatians were turning away from Christ:

> I marvel that you are turning away so soon from Him who called you in the grace of Christ to a different gospel (Galatians 1:6).

The Corinthian believers as well had all been baptized with the Holy Spirit but the Corinthians were guilty of all kinds of evils. The Apostle Paul told them:

And I, brethren, could not speak to you as spiritual people but as to carnal, as to babes in Christ . . . For you are still carnal. For where there are . . . divisions among you, are you not carnal and behaving like mere men? (1 Corinthians 3:1,3)

Therefore, we can say that the act of baptism with the Holy Spirit provides the basis for power by placing the believer into the body of Christ but does not guarantee any special power or ability to live the Christian life. That comes through obedience to God and being continually filled with the Holy Spirit.

WHAT IS THE FILLING OF THE HOLY SPIRIT?

One of the most important ministries of the Holy Spirit is that of filling of the believer, The filling of the Spirit gives the believer power to live the Christian life. The believer is commanded to be filled with the Holy Spirit:

And do not be drunk with wine, in which is dissipation; but be filled with the Spirit (Ephesians 5:18).

The filling of the Holy Spirit is not something that is merely suggested by God; it is a command. All believers are to be filled with the Holy Spirit. The filling of the Holy Spirit is contrasted with drunkenness. The idea behind each concept is control. While the effects of alcohol control the drunken person the effects of the Holy Spirit control the believer. Thus, when we speak of being filled with the Holy Spirit, we are speaking of being controlled by the Holy Spirit.

The filling as contrasted with other ministries of the Spirit, is directly experienced. It is a repeated experience. The command in Ephesians 5:18 is for the believer to be continually filled with the Holy Spirit.

We conclude regarding the filling of the Holy Spirit:

1. The Bible commands the believer to be filled with the Spirit.

2. The idea behind is control. God wants His people to be controlled by the Holy Spirit.

3. The filling of the Holy Spirit is a ministry of the Spirit that is directly experienced by the believer.

4. The filling of the Holy Spirit is a repeated experience.

IS THE BAPTISM WITH THE SPIRIT THE SAME AS THE FILLING OF THE SPIRIT?

When the Bible speaks of the baptism and the filling of the Holy Spirit, is it speaking of the same thing? Though people often speak of both as the same experience, the Bible makes a distinction between the two.

The baptism with the Holy Spirit takes place at the moment of salvation and places believers into the body of Christ. The filling of the Holy Spirit is something that occurs repeatedly after the person is saved. The baptism with the Holy Spirit is nonrepeatable. No one is ever spoken of receiving the baptism with the Spirit more than once. The filling of the Holy Spirit, on the other hand, is something that occurs many times. We see this in the life of the apostles:

> And they were all filled with the Holy Spirit and began to speak with other tongues, as the Spirit gave them utterance (Acts 2:4).

Yet these same disciples were filled again with the Holy Spirit:

> And when they had prayed, the place where they were assembled together was shaken; and they were all filled with the Holy Spirit (Acts 4:31).

The baptism with the Holy Spirit is a positional work that places a person in the body of Christ. The filling of the Spirit is an experiential work that has to do with living a Christian life.

What Happened at Pentecost?

If the baptism and the filling are two different ministries of the Holy Spirit, what happened on the Day of Pentecost? The Scriptures seem to speak of them as the same experience. Jesus made the following promise to the believers before He ascended into heaven:

> For John truly baptized with water, but you shall be baptized with the Holy Spirit not many days from now (Acts 1:5).

On the Day of Pentecost this promise was fulfilled:

> And they were all filled with the Holy Spirit and began to speak with other tongues, as the Spirit gave them utterance (Acts 2:4).

Same Experience?

Does this make the two the same experience? No. On the Day of Pentecost the believers were both baptized and filled with the Holy Spirit. The baptism with the Spirit is what joined them to Christ and provided the basis for their spiritual power. The filling of the Holy Spirit was the experience of that power. When the Bible records that they were filled with the Holy Spirit, it demonstrates that the baptism with the Holy Spirit had occurred.

Summary

In summary, the baptism and filling of the Holy Spirit are two separate ministries of the Spirit that occurred on the Day of Pentecost. Because the believers were baptized with the Holy Spirit, they were able to receive the Spirit's filling.

We can sum up the difference as follows:

1. The baptism with the Spirit occurs once at salvation, the filling of the Holy Spirit occurs after the believer is saved.

2 The baptism with the Holy Spirit occurs only once, while the filling of the Spirit occurs many times.

3 The baptism with the Holy Spirit is a positional work and is not directly experienced while the believer directly experiences the filling of the Spirit.

WHY DID PETER AND JOHN LAY HANDS ON THE SAMARITANS TO HAVE THEM RECEIVE THE HOLY SPIRIT?

There is an episode in the Book of Acts that seems to teach that the Holy Spirit was not given immediately at the point of salvation, but rather following it:

> Now when the apostles who were at Jerusalem heard that Samaria had received the word of God, they sent Peter and John to them, who, when they had come down, prayed for them that they might receive the Holy Spirit. For as yet He had fallen on none of them. They had only been baptized in the name of the Lord Jesus. Then they laid hands on them and they received the Holy Spirit (Acts 8:14-17).

Does not this delay prove that the Holy Spirit is given subsequent to salvation? The fact that there was a delay in the Samaritans' receiving the Holy Spirit after they were saved is clearly taught. If everyone receives the Holy Spirit upon being saved, why was there a delay in this case?

The best explanation of this occurrence has to do with the special nature of the Samaritan religion and its relationship to the Jews. The Samaritans had their own religious system that was a rival to the Jews. They had their own temple and their own center of worship. The two groups did not interact. "For Jews have no dealings with the Samaritans" (John 4:9).

Identify with Apostles

It was important for the Samaritans who believed in Christ to identify with the apostles in Jerusalem. Likewise, it was important for the Jewish element to see that the Samaritans were part of the same body of Christ. When the Holy Spirit was given by the laying on of hands of Peter and John, who were personal disciples of Jesus Christ and the leaders in the Jerusalem church, there was no doubt that these two groups were one in Christ. This delay in the Samaritans' receiving the Holy Spirit kept the early church from having two centers of authority, Samaria and Jerusalem.

The fact that the norm for the New Testament was the immediate reception of the Holy Spirit show that this was a special occurrence and not to be considered the pattern for every believer.

WHAT HAPPENED WHEN THE GENTILES FIRST RECEIVED THE HOLY SPIRIT?

For the first few years of the church's existence, only Jews believed in Jesus as their Savior. But Jesus had promised that His message would go out to all the world.

But you shall receive power when the Holy Spirit has come upon you; and you shall be witnesses to Me in Jerusalem, and in all Judea and Samaria, and to the end of the earth (Acts 1:8).

In Acts 10, the Gentiles (non-Jews) received the Holy Spirit. The first Gentile believers were Cornelius and his family. When the word was preached to them by Simon Peter, a personal disciple of Jesus Christ and a leader of the church, they believed the message.

While Peter was still speaking these words, the Holy Spirit fell upon all those who heard the word. And those of the circumcision who believe were astonished, as many as came with Peter, because the gift of the Holy Spirit had been poured out on the Gentiles also. For they heard them speak with tongues and magnify God. Then Peter answered, 'Can anyone forbid water, that these should not be baptized who have received the Holy Spirit just as we have' (Acts 10:44-47).

There are those who point to this passage as another indication of the gift of tongues as the sign of receiving the Holy Spirit. But this is not the case. In this instance, the tongue-speaking of the Gentiles convinced Peter and the other Jews that Gentiles were now part of the Christian church. Because the Gentiles exhibited the same supernatural ability to speak in tongues as the Jews did on the Day of Pentecost, it was clear that they too had received the Holy Spirit.

When Peter later recounted the story, the Jews rejoiced.

When they heard these things, they became silent; and they glorified God saying, 'Then God has also granted to the Gentiles repentance to life' (Acts 11:18).

The sign of tongues in this case, then, was to believing Jews to show them that God also had granted forgiveness of sins to Gentiles as well as to Jews.

WHY DID THE APOSTLE PAUL ASK CERTAIN DISCIPLES IF THEY RECEIVED THE HOLY SPIRIT UPON BELIEVING?

In Acts 19 we find the Apostle Paul asking certain disciples,

'Did you receive the Holy Spirit when you believed?' And they said to him, 'We have not so much as heard whether there is a Holy Spirit' (Acts 19:1).

The King James Version reads: "Have you received the Holy Spirit since you believed?" However, this is a poor translation of the Greek text which literally reads, "Having believed did you receive the Holy Spirit?"

Does this account indicate that there is a period of time between salvation and the reception of the Holy Spirit?

Again, when we understand the situation, we find that this is not the case. These disciples were followers of John the Baptist. Paul, noticing something lacking in their knowledge of Christ, asked them if they received the Holy Spirit when they believed John's message. Had they been baptized into Christ, they would have been familiar with the Trinitarian baptismal formula.

Go therefore and make disciples of all the nations, baptizing them in the name of the Father and of the Son and of the Holy Spirit (Matthew 28:19).

They confessed that they were ignorant of the Holy Spirit. These disciples had heard only John's message of the coming Messiah. They were ignorant of the fact of the death and resurrection of Jesus. Thus, the reason they had not received the Holy Spirit is that they were not Christians. When Paul then explained to them about the death and resurrection of Christ, they became believers and immediately received the Holy Spirit. So this was not a case of receiving the Holy Spirit after salvation but rather the reception of the Holy Spirit at salvation.

22

WHY DID THE HOLY SPIRIT WORK DIFFERENTLY WITH FOUR PARTICULAR GROUPS IN ACTS?

The Book of Acts represents a transitional time during which the Old Testament age was ending and the New Testament church age was beginning. It describes certain events that happened but does not explain their significance.

Throughout the New Testament, however, we learn certain things about the Holy Spirit. For example, He indwells every believer at the moment of salvation.

> In Him you also trusted, after you heard the word of truth, the gospel of your salvation; in whom also, having believed, you were sealed with the Holy Spirit of promise, who is the guarantee of our inheritance until the redemption of the purchased possession, to the praise of His glory (Ephesians 1:13,14).

Yet, in the Book of Acts, there are four instances of believers who received the Holy Spirit in a unique way. These were the disciples of Jesus, the Samaritans, the Gentiles, and the disciples of John the Baptist. These groups, as we have seen, received the Holy Spirit in varying ways because of the transition of the church and because the four groups represented all of humanity.

The people living at the time of Christ were in a transitional period. The Old Testament age of adherence to the law was ending, and the New Testament age of grace was beginning. God was now dealing in a different way with those who believed in Him. Although in every age people have been saved by the grace of God through faith in His promises, there were different methods God used in testifying to Himself.

These four groups in the Book of Acts represent all of humanity.

The Disciples of Jesus

The disciples of Jesus were one such group they had received the Holy Spirit in the upper room:

> And when He had said this, He breathed on them, and said to them, 'Receive the Holy Spirit' (John 20:22).

They were still living in the Old Testament age. At Pentecost, the disciples received the promise of the power and indwelling of the Holy Spirit. They represented those people who believed in Jesus while He was here upon the earth.

Samaritans

The Samaritans were half-Jewish, half-Gentile. They had their own religion, which was in conflict with Judaism. The reason they experienced the reception of the Holy Spirit apart from their salvation was to identify them with the Jews as being united in the new faith, Christianity. When they received the Holy Spirit through the laying on of hands of Peter and John, it demonstrated that both Jews and Samaritans were united in Christ.

Gentiles

A third class of humanity was the Gentiles (non-Jews). There was much racial prejudice between the Jews and Gentiles. By receiving the Holy Spirit with the disciples of Jesus it showed the unity between the two groups. The Apostle Paul would later write:

> There is neither Jew nor Greek, there is neither male nor female; for you are all one in Christ Jesus (Galatians 3:27).

Old Testament Believers

The last group were the believers who lived during the Old Testament period, waiting for the coming Messiah. They were signified by those who were disciples of John the Baptist, who received the Holy Spirit when they believed in Jesus as their Messiah.

The record of these four groups receiving salvation fulfills the prophecy spoken by Jesus:

> But you shall receive power when the Holy Spirit has come upon you; and you shall be witnesses to Me in Jerusalem, and in all Judea and Samaria, and to the end of the earth (Acts 1:8).

Throughout Scripture, we see that the New Testament pattern is for every believer to receive the Holy Spirit upon conversion. But because of the transitional nature of the time, the four groups of humanity each received the Holy Spirit in a unique way. This demonstrates that all people are one when they believe in Christ.

DOES THE BOOK OF ACTS PROVIDE ANY PATTERN FOR BELIEVERS TO RECEIVE THE HOLY SPIRIT?

Often people will speak of the "Acts pattern" for receiving the Holy Spirit. Supposedly the Book of Acts presents certain stages the believer must go through to receive the Holy Spirit and to speak with tongues. But when one examines the Book of Acts, no such pattern emerges.

Pentecost

On the day of Pentecost (Acts 2) the believers, who had been baptized, received the Holy Spirit and spoke in tongues without the laying on of hands.

Samaria

In Samaria (Acts 8) the people believe in Jesus and were baptized. Yet they did not receive the Holy Spirit until Peter and John came down and laid hands on them. There is no record that they spoke in tongues.

Gentiles

In Acts 10, the Holy Spirit fell upon the Gentiles while they were listening to the word. The Gentiles then spoke with tongues and were soon baptized. There was no laying on of hands in this case.

Disciples of John

In Acts 19, the disciples of John the Baptist believed and were baptized. The Holy Spirit then came upon them when Paul laid his hands upon them and they spoke in tongues.

When we look at these four instances of the unique reception of the Holy Spirit in the Book of Acts, no pattern emerges:

Acts 2:   received the Holy Spirit, spoke in tongues

Acts 8:   baptized with water, hands laid on them, received the Spirit

Acts 10:   received the Holy Spirit, spoke with tongues, baptized with water

Acts 19:   baptized with water, hands laid on them, received the Spirit, spoke with tongues

In these recorded instances all the experiences were different. Not all spoke in tongues, not everyone had hands laid upon them.

Thus, any pattern one tries to read into these accounts cannot be justified biblically. The Holy Spirit came down differently each time, reminding us of those words spoken by Jesus:

The wind blows where it wishes, and you hear the sound of it, but cannot tell where it comes from or where it goes. So is everyone who is born of the Spirit (John 3:8).

WHY DID JESUS BREATHE UPON HIS DISCIPLES TO RECEIVE THE HOLY SPIRIT?

We know that the Holy Spirit came upon Jesus' disciples on the Day of Pentecost. But the Scripture indicates that they had received the Holy Spirit before that time:

> Then Jesus said to them again, 'Peace to you! As the Father has sent Me, I also send you.' And when He had said this, He breathed on them and said to them, 'Receive the Holy Spirit' (John 20:21,22).

Does this indicate that there is a gap of time between receiving the Holy Spirit and experiencing His fullness?

Disciples Regenerated

Some feel the disciples were saved or regenerated at this time. The baptism with the Holy Spirit, which occurred on the Day of Pentecost, is viewed as a second work of the Spirit. But we have seen that the Bible does not teach that the baptism with the Holy Spirit is an experience subsequent to salvation.

Prophecy

Others take this statement of Jesus as a prophecy. When He said, "Receive the Holy Spirit," He was promising the disciples the Holy Spirit, which they received on the Day of Pentecost. The text, however, seems to state that the disciples received the Holy Spirit at that time, not just the promise of the Spirit.

Temporary Giving

A third viewpoint is to understand this as a temporary giving of the Spirit. The disciples were given this temporary infusion to last until the Day of Pentecost, when the Spirit came upon the believer permanently. This seems the best way to understand what occurred.

We conclude that this experience was unique to Jesus' disciples and does not serve as a pattern for the lives of present-day believers.

HOW DID THE HOLY SPIRIT SPEAK TO THE APOSTLES?

The Bible lists three instances in which the Holy Spirit spoke to the apostles.

As they ministered to the Lord and fasted, the Holy Spirit said, 'Now separate to Me Barnabas and Saul for the work which I have called them' (Acts 13:2).

How did He do it? How did He call Saul and Barnabas to special missionary service? The answer is we are not told, and we simply do not know. It was most likely through the means of a special revelation to one of the three teachers who remained. It is also possible that Saul himself received the revelation. The special revelation could have consisted of a vision, a verbal command, or the still small voice of the Holy Spirit.

We have similar accounts where the Holy Spirit is said to have spoken:

Now when they had gone through Phrygia and the region of Galatia, they were forbidden by the Holy Spirit to preach the word in Asia. After they had come to Mysia, they tried to go to Bithynia, but the Spirit did not permit them (Acts 16:6,7).

And see, now I go bound in the spirit to Jerusalem, not knowing the things that happen to me there, except that the Holy Spirit testifies in every city, saying that chains and tribulations await me (Acts 20:22,23).

Once again, we are not told how the Spirit spoke, only that He did speak.

Thus, we know that the Holy Spirit spoke to the apostles, but we are not told how He spoke to them.

WAS THE HOLY SPIRIT INVOLVED IN HELPING TO FORM THE NEW TESTAMENT?

One of the many ministries of the Holy Spirit was the formation of the New Testament. This is evident in a number of Scripture passages. First, Jesus promised that the Holy Spirit would guide the believer.

However when He, the Spirit of truth has come, He will guide you into all truth (John 16:13).

Jesus also promised that the Holy Spirit would give the disciples total recall of His words and deeds.

But the Helper, the Holy Spirit, whom the Father will send in My name, He will teach you all things, and bring to your remembrance all things that I said to you (John 14:26).

These are the same disciples who either wrote the New Testament or had control over which books were recognized as inspired by God. The Holy Spirit supernaturally guided their finished product.

This guaranteed that the contents of the New Testament, as was true with the Old Testament, were protected by God. The Bible says,

Knowing this first, that no prophecy of Scripture is of any private interpretation, for prophecy never came by the will of man, but holy men of God spoke as they were moved by the Holy Spirit (2 Peter 1:20,21).

The Bible also says:

All Scripture is given by inspiration of God, and is profitable for doctrine, for reproof, for correction, for instruction in righteousness (2 Timothy 3:16).

We see in Scripture that the Holy Spirit helped form the New Testament in three ways. First, Jesus promised that the Spirit would guide all believers (and the disciples specifically) into all truth. Also, the Spirit helped the apostles remember Jesus' words and the events of His life. Finally, the Spirit guided the apostles and others in determining the content of the Bible as God's authoritative Word to believers.

WHAT IS THE MINISTRY OF THE HOLY SPIRIT TO THE UNBELIEVING WORLD?

The Bible teaches that the Holy Spirit has a ministry not only to the believer but also to the unbelieving world.

Jesus, in talking to His disciples, revealed to them the Holy Spirit's ministry to the world:

> Nevertheless I tell you the truth. It is to your advantage that I go away; for if I do not go away, the Helper will not come to you; but if I depart, I will send Him to you. And when He has come, He will convict the world of sin, and of righteousness, and of judgment: of sin, because they do not believe in Me; of righteousness, because I go to My Father and you will see me no more; of judgment, because the ruler of this world is judged (John 16:7-11)

The Holy Spirit has a personal ministry in the life of each individual unbeliever. He convicts them of sin and their need to receive Christ as Savior. The sin that the Holy Spirit convicts the world of is not any one specific sin, but the one that will keep them from getting to heaven—the sin of unbelief.

> And this is the condemnation, that light has come into the world, and men loved darkness rather than light, because their deeds were evil (John 3:19).

Jesus said the Holy Spirit convicts people of sin because they reject Him: "Because they do not believe in Me" (John 16:9).

The remedy is for the unbeliever to recognize his sin of unbelief and trust Christ as Savior. Each individual chooses whether to accept or reject the Holy Spirit's conviction.

Denial of Righteousness

The Holy Spirit also convicts the world for denying God's righteousness. God's righteousness is offended by the continual sin of the individual. The Bible speaks of the unbeliever as suppressing the truth of God in unrighteousness:

> For the wrath of God is revealed from heaven against all ungodliness and unrighteousness of men, who suppress the truth of God in unrighteousness (Romans 1:18).

The thought behind this verse is that the unbelieving person is willfully suppressing the truth of God that is trying to reach him. The Holy Spirit is convicting each unbelieving individual for doing this.

Judgment

Finally, the Holy Spirit convicts the world by judgment. One reason for the coming of Christ was to destroy the works of the devil:

> For this purpose the Son of God was manifested, that He might destroy the works of the devil (1 John 3:8).

Jesus lived a perfect, sinless life, and His death upon the cross paid the price for every person's sins. When He rose three days later, not only had sin been defeated, but death also.

The ministry of the Holy Spirit to the unbeliever is to reveal the truth that God indeed is victorious in the conflict with the devil, and the unbelieving world no longer has to live in the grip of Satan.

Restrainer

The Holy Spirit also has a ministry to the world as a restrainer. As bad as things are in the world, they would be much worse without the restraining influence of the Holy Spirit. The Holy Spirit is presently acting as a restraining force to hold back sin. He does this through the influence of the believer. As long as the Holy Spirit is working in the world through the presence of the believer, sin will not run utterly rampant.

In this way, the Holy Spirit ministers to the world. He also does this, as we have seen, by convicting the world of its sin, by revealing its need for Christ's salvation, and by restraining evil.

WILL THE HOLY SPIRIT BE AT WORK DURING THE GREAT TRIBULATION?

There has been much discussion as to how the Holy Spirit will work during the seven year period of tribulation that will occur in the future. Will He be absent? Will He work in the same way as today?

The Bible indicates that the Holy Spirit will be active during this period, and as a result multitudes will be converted. The Scripture mentions three specific groups: the 144,000, a great multitude, and Jews who have passed through God's judgment.

The 144,000

At the beginning of this period, the 144,000 Jews will be converted and sealed, or protected, by the Holy Spirit.

> And I heard the number of those who were sealed. One hundred and forty-four thousand of all the tribes of the children of Israel were sealed . . . These were redeemed among men, being firstfruits of God and to the lamb (Revelation 7:4,14:4).

After they are saved, they become witnesses of Jesus Christ to the remainder of mankind.

Great Multitude

The Bible testifies that an innumerable multitude will be converted out of the Great Tribulation:

> After these things I looked and behold, a great multitude which no one could number, of all the nations, tribes, people, and tongues, standing before the throne and before the Lamb, clothed with white robes, with palm branches in their hands, and crying out with a loud voice, saying, 'Salvation belongs to our God who sits on the throne, and to the Lamb' (Revelation 7:9,10).

Jewish Believers

The Holy Spirit will be at work through a third group of people who are converted. These are Jewish believers who have survived the judgment of the great tribulation:

> And I will pour on the house of David and on the inhabitants of Jerusalem the Spirit of grace and supplication; then they will look on Me whom they have pierced; they will mourn for Him as one who grieves for a firstborn (Zechariah 12:10).

The work of the Holy Spirit will not cease during this period. On the contrary, many unbelievers will come to know Jesus Christ through the Spirit's work.

HOW WILL THE HOLY SPIRIT WORK DURING THE MILLENNIUM?

The millennial reign of Christ will last for one thousand years. It will occur after His second coming. During this time peace will rule. How will the Holy Spirit function during this period? Will there still be the need for people to be converted?

Those who survived the Great Tribulation and have not believed in Him will be judged by Christ at His second coming before the Millennium begins. When the millennium begins, all those who enter into it will be believers. Both Jews and Gentiles who have survived the Great Tribulation with faith in Christ will enter this period.

Judgment on Gentiles

Jesus talked about the this judgment of the unbelieving Gentiles.

When the Son of Man comes in His glory, and all the holy angels with Him, then He will set on the throne of His glory. All the nations will be gathered before Him, and He will separate them one from another, as a shepherd divides his sheep from the goats. And He will set the sheep on His right hand, but the goats on the left. Then the king will say to those on His right hand, 'Come, you blessed of My Father, inherit the kingdom prepared for you from the foundation of the world.' . . . Then He will also say to those on the left hand, 'Depart from Me, you cursed, into everlasting fire prepared for the devil and his angels' (Matthew 25:31-34,41).

Judgment of the Jews

The prophet Zechariah spoke of the judgment of the Jews:

And it shall come to pass in all the land,' says the Lord, 'That two thirds in it shall be cut off and die, but one third shall be left in it. I will bring the one third through the fire, will refine them as silver is refined, and test them as gold is tested. They will call upon My name and I will answer them. I will say, 'This is My people;' And each will say, 'The Lord is my God!' (Zechariah 13:8,9).

Those that survive these two judgments will enter the millennial period. Therefore all those who begin the Millennium are believers.

However, children will be born during this period, and each of them will need to make a personal decision toward Christ. The Holy Spirit will be working in their lives to bring them into a relationship with God. Yet, despite the Holy Spirit's work, there will be those who reject Christ:

Now when the thousand years have expired, Satan will be released from prison and will go out to deceive the nations which are in the four corners of the earth, Gog and Magog, to gather them into battle, whose number is as the sand of the sea. They went on the breadth of the earth and surrounded the camp of the saints and the beloved city. And fire came down from God out of heaven and devoured them (Revelation 20:7-9).

Therefore, we see the need for the Holy Spirit to work during the Millennium in the lives of unbelievers.

CONCLUSION TO PART 2

The Bible has much to say about the works the Holy Spirit has performed:

1.   The Bible attributes many works to the Holy Spirit. They include the creation, upholding, and running of the universe.

2.   The Holy Spirit works as He wills. He is likened to the wind which is powerful though invisible.

3.   The Holy Spirit was at work during the Old Testament period, guiding people for service.

4.   The Holy Spirit was involved in the life of Christ from His birth until His death.

5.   The Holy Spirit came down in a unique way on the Day of Pentecost.

6.   The Holy Spirit baptizes believers into the body of Christ.

7.   The Holy Spirit indwells each individual who believes in Jesus.

8.   The Book of Acts provides no set pattern as to how the Holy Spirit will work in the life of the believer.

9.   The Holy Spirit worked in a unique way with four classes of people in the Book of Acts so that they could be united in Christ.

10. The Holy Spirit was intimately involved with the formation of the Old and New Testament. He has helped guarantee its accuracy.

11. The Holy Spirit will be at work during the period of great tribulation on the earth.

12. The Holy Spirit will have a ministry during the one thousand year millennial reign of Christ.

PART 3

THE GIFTS OF THE HOLY SPIRIT

WHAT ARE
SPIRITUAL GIFTS?

Before we examine the subject of spiritual gifts, we need to have an understanding of what they are. Though the Bible does not give a definition of spiritual gifts, it does tell us much regarding their nature and function. The word normally translated "gift" in the New Testament is the Greek word *charismata*. The word means "gifts of grace" and refers to the gifts or special abilities God has given believers through the Holy Spirit.

Not the Holy Spirit

Spiritual gifts, or the gifts of the Holy Spirit, are not the same as the gift of the Holy Spirit. There are many gifts of the Spirit, but there is only one Holy Spirit. The gift of the Holy Spirit is received the moment a person trusts Christ as Savior. Simon Peter said to the multitude on the Day of Pentecost:

> Repent, and let every one of you be baptized in the name of Jesus Christ for the remission of sins; and you shall receive the gift of the Holy Spirit (Acts 2:38).

Not Human Talents

Spiritual gifts are abilities God gives the believer for the purpose of service. They are not human talents. Human talents are inadequate to do the work of God.

For though we walk in the flesh, we do not war
according to the flesh. For the weapons of our warfare are
not carnal but mighty in God for pulling down
strongholds (2 Corinthians 10:3,4).

Spiritual gifts are either supernatural abilities that God
has bestowed on individuals, or God-given natural abilities
that function through the direction of the Holy Spirit. Gifts
such as miracles, tongues, healing, and prophecy are
supernatural in origin. Other spiritual gifts, such as
teaching, administration, and helps, are God-given
abilities to perform a particular role in God's program.
Though nonbelievers may have the same abilities, they do
not function under the direction of the Holy Spirit. The
Holy Spirit takes these God-given abilities and uses them
for His purposes in the lives of believers. Therefore, the
gifts of the Spirit are abilities, either natural or
supernatural, given by God for the work of the ministry.
The Bible says that all gifts ultimately have their
source in God.

Every good gift and perfect gift is from above, and
comes down from the Father of lights, with whom there is
no variation or shadow of turning (James 1:17).

Not the Fruit of the Spirit

The gifts of the Spirit are not the same as the fruit of
the Spirit. The gifts of the Spirit have to do with service
while the fruit of the Spirit has to do with character.

But the fruit of the Spirit is love, joy, peace,
longsuffering, kindness, goodness, faithfulness,
gentleness, self-control. Against such there is no law
(Galatians 5:22,23).

Spiritual gifts are the means; spiritual fruit is the end.
Gifts are what the believer possesses, but the fruit of the
Spirit is what the believer becomes. Spiritual gifts will
someday cease, while spiritual fruits are permanent.

Gifts Are Not Offices

The gifts of the Holy Spirit are not the same as the
various offices mentioned in the New Testament: the office
of apostle, prophet, pastor, teacher, elder, and deacon.
Those who occupy such offices should possess the

THE GIFTS OF THE HOLY SPIRIT   101

spiritual gift that goes with it. Yet a person can have the gift—of prophecy or teaching, for example—without occupying the office of a prophet or teacher.

Classification of Gifts

The Bible lists the gifts of the Spirit in four different portions of Scripture: Romans 12:6-8, 1 Corinthians 12:4-11, 1 Corinthians 12:28, Ephesians 4:11. They have been classified in many different ways, but we will examine them in three groups:

1. Ministering Gifts: The gifts of an apostle, evangelist, pastor, teacher, exhorter, and discerner of spirits; the word of wisdom and the word of knowledge.

2. Serving Gifts: The gifts of ministering, giving, ruling, showing mercy, and displaying faith.

3. Sign Gifts. The gifts of prophecy, healing, miracles, tongues, and interpreting tongues.

These gifts are not necessarily in order from the greater to the lesser. Some of the gifts overlap, and this list is not meant to be taken as complete. There may be many more spiritual gifts than these listed here.

We conclude concerning spiritual gifts:

1. A spiritual gift is a supernatural ability given by God to the believer for the purpose of serving.

2. A spiritual gift may be a God-given talent that is directed by the Holy Spirit. It is not a mere human talent.

3. A spiritual gift is not the same as the gift of the Spirit.

4. Spiritual gifts are not the same as the fruit of the Spirit.

5. The Bible teaches that the offices of the Holy Spirit are different from the gifts of the Spirit. A person may possess a gift without holding the corresponding office.

6. The Bible lists about twenty spiritual gifts but there may be many more. Every believer has a spiritual gift.

WHAT DOES THE BIBLE HAVE TO SAY ABOUT THE CHRISTIAN AND SPIRITUAL GIFTS?

The Bible includes many references regarding the believer and spiritual gifts. From these passages we learn the following:

Every Believer Has a Gift

Every Christian has at least one spiritual gift:

As each one has received a gift, minister it to one another, as stewards of the manifold grace of God (1 Peter 4:10).

But to each one of us grace was given according to the measure of Christ's gift (Ephesians 4:7).

A believer may not know what his spiritual gift is, but he has one regardless of whether he exercises it. There are no ungifted believers.

For Others Benefit

The purpose of the gifts are to build up and encourage other believers. They are not for pride or individual glory.

But are manifestations of the Spirit is given to each one for the profit of all (1 Corinthians 12:7).

God Gives the Gifts

God is the source of all spiritual gifts. The Bible teaches that each member of the Trinity is involved in giving spiritual gifts.

God has dealt to each a measure of faith (Romans 12:3).

But one and the same Spirit works all these things, distributing to each other individually as He wills (1 Corinthians 12:11).

But to each one of us grace was given according to the measure of Christ's gift. Therefore He says, 'When He ascended on high, He led captivity captive, and gave gifts to men' (Ephesians 4:7,8).

We cannot earn a gift through human effort. Spiritual gifts are not rewards for diligence. No one should boast or be idolized for having a more prominent or visible gift. The gifts do not represent a degree of spiritual growth. They are given by God to certain believers as He desires.

The Gifts are Varied

There are a variety of gifts, and the Apostle Paul likens them to the components of a human body.

But now God has set the members each one of them, in the body just as He pleased. And if they were all one member, where would the body be? But now indeed there are many members, yet one body (1 Corinthians 12:18-20).

Every believer has a gift, but no believer has all the gifts. Each member of the body needs the other; there are no unimportant spiritual gifts.

Desire the Best Gifts

It is not for us to say which gifts we can have; God is the one who gives the gifts. Yet, the Bible encourages us to desire the best gifts:

But earnestly desire the best gifts (1 Corinthians 12:31).

Though we should desire the best gifts, we do not have a right to insist upon them. God is the giver of the gifts.

Gifts Can be Developed

The gift of teaching, for instance, is a supernatural ability given by God to teach His Word. This gift can be developed as the believer takes time to study and learn the things of God. Certain gifts can and should be developed.

Gifts Need to be Used

After discussing the gifts of the Spirit, the Apostle Paul said, "Let us use them" (Romans 12:6). The Bible encourages the believer to be faithful to the gifts God has given him:

As each one has received a gift, minister it to one another, as good stewards of the manifold grace of God (1 Peter 4:10).

Moreover it is required in stewards that one be found faithful (1 Corinthians 4:2).

Gifts also need to be rekindled, or exercised when they are not used regularly.

Therefore I remind you to stir up the gift of God which is in you through the laying on of my hands (2 Timothy 1:6).

Therefore we can conclude the following regarding the believer and spiritual gifts:

1. Every believer has a spiritual gift.

2. The gifts are given by God to build up the body of Christ.

3. The gifts are given by God as He wills.

4. Every believer has a gift but no believer has all the gifts.

5. Certain of the gifts can be developed through time.

6. Gifts need to be used. They should be rekindled if they are not being used.

WHAT IS THE GIFT OF AN APOSTLE?

One of the most important spiritual gifts listed is the gift of an apostle.

And God has appointed these in the church: first apostles (1 Corinthians 12:28).

The word apostle comes from the Greek word *apostolos* and means "one who is sent."

Introduces the Message

The gift of apostle is the special ability to introduce the message of Christ to a particular group, perhaps a different culture, and then to disciple those who have believed. An apostle is a church planter or missionary, though his ministry does not have to be in a foreign country.

The office of apostle was foundational to the church:

Having been built on the foundation of apostles and prophets, Jesus Christ Himself being the chief cornerstone (Ephesians 2:20).

The gift was given for the instruction and nurturing of believers. It is not the same gift as a pastor. A pastor performs his duties to only one congregation, while the apostle establishes and equips local assemblies of believers. However, an apostle can exercise the gift of pastor. He may start a church and remain there as pastor.

Cannot be Earned

Like other spiritual gifts, the gift of an apostle cannot be earned by merit. It is a God-given gift to perform the duties of a church planter, introducing the message of Christ to the unevangelized.

DO PEOPLE TODAY HAVE THE GIFT OF APOSTLE?

Is the gift of apostle still with the church today? There has been much discussion concerning the twelve original apostles and whether or not they were the only ones with this gift. In a particular sense, the office of apostle referred to the twelve disciples of Jesus:

> And when it was day, He called His disciples to Him; and from them He chose twelve whom He also named apostles (Luke 6:13).

One of the Twelve, Judas, was replaced after his suicide. However, the Twelve, as they are known, did not have successors.

But the New Testament uses the term *apostle* for others beside the original twelve. Paul was not one of the original twelve but he is called an apostle: Am I not an apostle?" (1 Corinthians 9:1).

Barnabas also served as an apostle:

> But when the apostles, Barnabas and Paul heard this (Acts 14:14).

The New Testament mentions additional apostles who were not among the Twelve: Andronicus, Junias (Romans 16:7), James the brother of Jesus (Galatians 1:19), Silvanus and Timothy (1 Thessalonians 1:1; 2:6).

Furthermore, the warning Paul gave concerning false apostles (2 Corinthians 11:13) would have no meaning if the apostles were limited to the Twelve. Thus the word *apostle* has both a limited and wide sense.

Though some believe the gift of being an apostle is no longer active among Christians, biblical evidence indicates that the gift continues:

> And He Himself gave some to be apostles (Ephesians 4:11).

WHAT IS THE GIFT OF PROPHECY?

In the New Testament the gift of prophecy is near the top of the list of spiritual gifts.

And God has appointed these in the church: first apostles, second prophets (1 Corinthians 12:29).

Pursue love, and desire spiritual gifts, but especially that you may prophesy (1 Corinthians 14:1).

The gift of prophecy is a special ability to speak forth the message of God. A prophet is basically a spokesman for God. He or she delivers the Word of God to people by means of direct revelation. Prophetic utterances can deal with certain individuals, the church, or a larger context. It does not always refer to the future.

In a general sense, a preacher who proclaims the Word of God acts in a prophetic role. He is speaking for God. But prophecy is not the same thing as preaching. Prophecy may involve foretelling something that will happen in the future. The New Testament gives an example of this:

Then one of them, named Agabus, stood up and showed by the Spirit that there was going to be a great famine throughout all the world, which also happened in the days of Claudius Caesar (Acts 11:28).

The gift of prophecy gave rise to the office or prophet in the early church. The Apostle Paul spoke of the apostles and prophets as God's gift to the church:

Having been built on the foundation of the apostles and prophets, Jesus Christ Himself being the chief cornerstone . . . And He Himself gave some to be apostles, some prophets, some evangelists, and some pastors and teachers (Ephesians 2:20;4:11).

Not all people with the gift of prophecy held the office of prophet, but those who held the prophetic office had the gift of prophecy. The Bible speaks of both men and women exercising the gift of prophecy:

Now this man had four virgin daughters who prophesied (Acts 21:9).

Now Judas and Silas, themselves being prophets also exhorted the brethren with many words and strengthened them (Acts 15:32).

Therefore, we conclude the following about the gift of prophecy:

1. The gift of prophecy is regarded as one of the best gifts.

2. A prophet is a spokesman for God.

3. The gift of prophecy consists of delivering a message from God which may involve a direct revelation.

4. The gift of prophecy may deal with predicting the future.

5. The office of prophet is the foundation upon which the church has been built.

6. Both men and women may exercise the gift of prophecy.

WHAT RULES DOES THE NEW TESTAMENT GIVE FOR PROPHESYING AT A WORSHIP SERVICE?

The Apostle Paul set down rules regarding prophesying at a worship service. He made it clear that these were rules set down by God.

If anyone things himself to be a prophet or spiritual, let him acknowledge that the things which I write to you are the commandments of the Lord (1 Corinthians 14:37).

Self-Control

The first rules states that the prophet must exercise self-control. Those who give prophetic utterances are not to act with uncontrolled frenzy:

But the fruit of the Spirit is . . . self-control (Galatians 5:22,23).

When the Spirit of God is working through one who prophesies, he will exercise self-restraint. Therefore, anyone who gets in an uncontrollable state when prophesying is not being led by the Spirit of God.

Limited Numbers

The second rule states that prophecies should be limited to two or three per meeting. "Let two or three prophets speak" (1 Corinthians 14:29).

Judged by Others

A third rule says the prophecies are to be judged by others in the assembly. The New Testament does not encourage believers to blindly follow anyone who claims to prophesy in the name of the Lord. When a prophet speaks, said the Apostle Paul, "Let the others judge" (1 Corinthians 14:29).

Consistent

Most important, the prophecies must be consistent with what God has already revealed. If a prophet brings forth a message that contradicts what the Scripture says, then we can be assured that the prophecy is not from God.

The Bible gives the following rules regarding prophetic utterances:

1. The prophet will be in control of his senses. He will not be in an uncontrolled state.

2. Prophecies are limited to two or three per meeting.

3. Prophecies are to be judged by others.

4. Any prophetic message given is to be in conformity with what God has already revealed.

HOW CAN WE TEST PROPHECIES?

If the gift of prophecy is to be exercised in the church today, believers must have guidelines to determine whether or not a particular prophetic utterance has come from God.

Conform to God's Word

The first thing that prophetic utterances should be tested by the revealed Word of God. Is the prophecy in harmony with Scripture? The Apostle John encourages us to test the prophets:

> Beloved, do not believe every Spirit, but test the spirits, whether they are of God; because many false prophets have gone out into the world (1 John 4:1).

Any alleged prophetic teaching that contradicts what God has previously revealed demonstrates itself to be from another source. Thus a prophetic utterance must first be in harmony with what God has previously revealed. The Bible says to be on guard against false prophecies.

> I marvel that you are turning away so soon from Him who called you in the grace of Christ, to a different gospel, which is not another; but there are some who trouble you and want to pervert the gospel of Christ. But even if we, or an angel from heaven, preach any other gospel to you

than what we have preached to you, let him be accursed (Galatians 1:6-8).

Testify to Jesus

The second test is similar to the first. The Scripture is clear that prophecy should reveal Jesus Christ:

For the testimony of Jesus is the spirit of prophecy (Revelation 19:10).

By this you know the Spirit of God: Every spirit that confesses that Jesus Christ has come in the flesh is of God, and every spirit that does not confess that Jesus Christ has come in the flesh is not of God (1 John 4:2,3).

Prophetic utterances should magnify Jesus Christ and Him alone. In addition, if the one giving the prophecy denies that Jesus was fully divine and fully human, then that person is a false prophet. Thus, the way the prophets view Jesus' character and teaching is another test that can be applied.

Moral Consistency

There is also a moral test that the prophet must pass. Is the person giving the prophecy exhibiting moral character consistent with his office? Jesus warned of these false prophets.

Beware of false prophets, who come in to you in sheep's clothing, but inwardly are ravenous wolves. You will know them by their fruits (Matthew 7:15,16).

The fruit that people exhibit is the fruit of their doctrine and the fruit of their lives. Both of these must be in harmony with God's Word. Does the prophet live a life glorifying to God? Is he in submission to the authority to God's Word? Those who do not conform to God's standards should not be regarded as prophets.

If, however, someone meets all these criteria, are we assume that their message is supernaturally given? Not necessarily. Apart from false prophecy, there are other types of messages that may seem worthy, but are not sent directly from God. Someone can meet all these criteria and give a message believing that it was from God, yet the source can be that professed prophet's own personality.

Leaders to Judge

The ones who are to judge whether a prophecy is God-given are the leaders in that particular assembly where the prophecy is uttered. The prophecies should not be spoken without the leaders commenting upon them. The basis of their judgment is a supernaturally given discernment by God.

The Bible says that prophetic utterances should be allowed in the churches. "Do not despise prophecies" (1 Thessalonians 5:20).

Prophecies should not be despised, but they should be tested. "Test all things; hold fast what is good" (1 Thessalonians 5:21).

Therefore, with regard to prophecy we can conclude:

1. A prophet must not contradict anything God has previously revealed.

2. A prophecy must exalt Jesus Christ.

3. A prophet's life must be consistent with the prophecy he or she gives.

4. Because someone meets the above criteria does not necessarily mean that the message is from God. The leaders of each particular assembly should be the ones who make the determination.

5. Prophecies should be tested, and if they hold true, they should not be despised.

ARE MODERN-DAY PROPHETIC UTTERANCES TO BE GIVEN THE SAME AUTHORITY AS SCRIPTURE?

When someone gives a prophecy invoking the name of the Lord are we to place it on the same level as Scripture? Though some modern-day prophecies may prove to be supernaturally given and helpful to those who receive them, they are not to be placed on the same level as the Bible.

Difference in Scope

The difference between modern-day prophetic utterances and Scripture is a matter of scope. The words set down in the Bible have a universal and eternal application. Those who have a genuine message from the Lord will have its application in a limited and often localized application. Such messages relate to individuals or a small number of people and are not to be placed on the same level as Scripture. This is because the Scriptures are complete. The faith has been once-and-for-all revealed to us by God and nothing further needs to be added. (For more information that the Bible is now complete, see Don Stewart, *What Everyone Needs To Know About The Bible*, Orange, California, Dart Press, 1992).

WHAT IS THE PASTORAL GIFT?

According to the Bible, the abilities of a pastor are spiritual gifts:

And He Himself gave some to be . . . pastors (Ephesians 4:1).

A pastor is supernaturally called by God to oversee a group of believers. The pastor is to be the teaching elder. In the New Testament he is also called "shepherd," or "bishop." He is to teach and guide the congregation.

Shepherd the flock of God which is among you, serving as overseers, not by constraint but willingly, not for dishonest gain but eagerly; not as being lords over those entrusted to you, but being examples to the flock (1 Peter 5:23).

Jesus said to His disciples, "Feed My lambs" (John 21:16).

Qualifications

The Apostle Paul wrote some of the qualifications of a pastor.

For a bishop must be blameless, as a steward of God, not self-willed, not quick-tempered, not given to wine, not violent, not greedy for money, but hospitable, a lover of what is good, sober-minded, just, holy, self-controlled, holding fast the faithful word as he has been taught, that he may be able, by sound doctrine, both to exhort and convict those who contradict (Titus 1:6-8).

Simply put, a pastor is to minister to the needs of a group of believers.

WHAT IS THE GIFT OF TEACHING?

God has given certain people the gift of teaching.

And God has appointed these in the church; first apostles, second prophets, third teachers (1 Corinthians 12:28).

And He Himself gave some to be . . . teachers (Ephesians 4:11).

The gift of teaching is a God-given ability to properly interpret and explain God's Word to others. It is something given with the gift of being a pastor, but it is not the same gift. A teacher can be a pastor but he does not necessarily have to be.

Essential

Proper teaching is essential to the life and service of the church. Jesus instructed us to love God with all our minds.

You shall love the Lord your God with all your heart, with all your soul, and with all your mind (Matthew 22:37).

We must have sound teaching to be able to do this.

The gift of teaching was an essential part of the early church. The Bible says of the Apostle Paul:

And he continued there a year and six months, teaching the word of God among them (Acts 18:11).

The Apostle Paul taught young Timothy so that he could teach others.

A husband and wife, Aquila and Priscilla, taught Apollos, a man mighty in the Scriptures, so he also could teach others:

So he [Apollos] began to speak boldly in the synagogue. When Aquila and Priscilla heard him, they took him aside and explained to him the way of God more accurately (Acts 18:26).

Teaching was crucial to the early church.

The Bible also warns of the great responsibility of being a teacher:

My brethren, let not many of you become teachers, knowing that we shall receive the stricter judgment (James 3:1).

Though the gift of teaching is God-given, it can be developed by the individual. In fact, a person with the gift of teaching should spend time to become more learned in God's Word. Proper teaching is essential to the growth and development of the church.

WHAT IS THE GIFT OF ADMINISTRATION?

The Bible speaks of another God-given spiritual gift that can be developed—the gift of administration:

> And God has appointed these in the church . . . gifts of . . . administrations (1 Corinthians 12:28).

Administration involves the ability to rule in the church and to govern the things of God. Scripture points out that administrators—church leaders—are to be shepherds, not tyrants. John gives an example who did not exercise proper leadership:

> I wrote to the church, but Diotrephes, who loves to have the preeminence among them, does not receive us. Therefore, if I come, I will call to mind his deeds which he does, prating against us with malicious words. And not content with that, he himself does not receive the brethren, and forbids those who wish to, putting them out of the church (3 John 9,10).

Right leadership prevents disorders in the church:

> And we urge you, brethren, to recognize those who labor among you, and are over you in the Lord and admonish you (1 Thessalonians 5:12).

Peter encouraged the leadership to be examples:

Nor as being lords over those entrusted to you, but being examples to the flock (1 Peter 5:3).

Those who lead must be filled with the Holy Spirit.

Seek out from among you seven men of good reputation, full of the Holy Spirit and wisdom, whom we may appoint over business (Acts 6:3).

In listing the qualifications of a leader in 1 Timothy 3:1-13, the Apostle Paul included a warning:

Not a novice, lest being puffed up by pride he fall into the same condemnation as the devil (1 Timothy 3:6).

This warning is vital to church order. An individual may have the ability to administrate in business, but that does not mean that he can or should administrate in the church. God's ways are no the ways of the world, and certain practices that are routinely done in the business world have no place in the church. Moreover, a new believer should not be given the authority over ruling the things of God no matter how talented he may be in the business world.

Thus, an administrator has a gift that preserves order in the body of Christ. He must exercise the gift to rule the church as a leader, not as a tyrant. The gift can be developed, as should the administrator's growth as a Christian.

WHAT IS THE GIFT OF AN EVANGELIST?

The Bible speaks of evangelism as a spiritual gift:

> And He Himself gave some to be . . . evangelists (Ephesians 4:11).

The word *evangelism* comes from a Greek word meaning "to proclaim the good news." An evangelist has a particular gift in telling others the good news about Jesus Christ. The good news is that Jesus died for the sins of the world, was buried, and rose again from the third day; by doing this, He conquered sin and death. Evangelism consists of telling others the gospel story. It is not a "nonverbal witness." Evangelists proclaim the message to others.

All believers are commanded to evangelize.

> Go therefore and make disciples of all the nations, baptizing them in the name of the Father and of the Son and of the Holy Spirit (Matthew 28:19).

Although every believer is instructed to evangelize, some are specially gifted with this ability. The New Testament gives examples of those who have the gift:

> On the next day we who were Paul's companions departed and came to Caesarea, and entered the house of Philip the evangelist, who was one of the seven, and stayed with him (Acts 21:8).

Paul exhorted Timothy to exercise his gift of evangelism:

But you be watchful in all things, endure afflictions, do the work of an evangelist, fulfill your ministry (2 Timothy 4:5).

A person with the gift of evangelism does not necessarily have to exercise it before a large audience. It can be done on a one-on-one situation. Philip, the evangelist, did both public and personal evangelism (See Acts 8).

WHAT IS THE GIFT
OF EXHORTATION?

Another gift of the Holy Spirit is that of exhortation.

> Having then gifts differing according to the grace that
> is given to us, let us use them . . . he who exhorts, in
> exhortation (Romans 12:6,8).

The gift of exhortation is listed separately from the gift
of teaching. The word *exhortation* come from a root word
that means "to advocate or comfort." Exhortation is a gift
that enables a person to encourage others to become
mature in Christ. Those with the gift of exhortation will
attempt to bring out the best in people, to bring them to
spiritual maturity. Exhortation includes rebuking fellow
believers for their sins. It is not the same as teaching.

A teacher may have the gift of exhortation as did
Barnabas.

> And Joses, who is also named Barnabas . . . (which is
> translated Son of Encouragement) (Acts 4:36).

The Apostle Paul also possessed this gift. He and
Barnabas exhorted the believers.

> And when they had preached the gospel to that city
> and made many disciples, they returned to Lystra,
> Iconium, and Antioch, strengthening the souls of the
> disciples, exhorting them to continue in the faith (Acts
> 14:21,22).

Depending upon the circumstances, the gift of exhortation can encourage or rebuke the church. A teacher should possess this gift, but not all those with the gift are teachers.

WHAT IS THE
GIFT OF GIVING?

Giving is listed as a spiritual gift.

Having then gifts according to the grace that is given us, let us use them . . . he who gives, with liberality (Romans 12:6,8).

All believers are encouraged to be generous with their belongings.

So let each one give, as he purposes in his heart, not grudgingly or of necessity; for God loves a cheerful giver (2 Corinthians 9:7).

Heal the sick, cleanse the lepers, raise the dead, cast our demons. Freely you have received, freely give (Matthew 10:8).

Give, and it shall be given to you: good measure, pressed down, shaken together, and running over will be put into your bosom. For with the same measure that you use, it will be measured back to you (Luke 6:38).

Sacrificial Giving

There is, however, a spiritual gift of sacrificial giving. It involves the giving of one's own possessions, including money, to others. It is not to be done with the idea of gaining it back. There is to be no thought of a return on an

investment. It is not a spiritual gift reserved for the
wealthy. Anyone, no matter what his financial resources
may be, can have the gift of giving.

WHAT IS THE GIFT OF FAITH?

The Bible says that the spiritual gifts include a gift of faith: "To another faith by the same Spirit" (1 Corinthians 12:9).

All believers have a certain amount of faith that is a gift from God.

> For, I say, through the grace given to me, to everyone who is among you, not to think of himself more highly than he ought to think, but to think soberly, as God has dealt to each one a measure of faith (Romans 12:3).

There is a gift of faith, however, that is a special ability to trust God beyond the limits of what we think is normally possible. Not every believer possesses this gift.

An example of an individual who has exercised the gift of faith is George Muller. Muller lived in nineteenth-century England. He had a great desire to help orphans and spent his life educating them and building orphanages. By exercising the gift of faith, he was able to raise money, time and time again, for the needs of the orphans. Without ever appealing to man, Muller amazingly had his needs met.

The successful missionary William Carey said, "Attempt great things for God—expect great things from God." Those with the gift of faith are able to do this.

WHAT IS THE GIFT
OF MINISTERING?

The idea behind ministering is to serve. When Paul wrote to the Corinthians, he referred to this as the gift of helps.

And God has appointed these in the church . . . gifts of . . . helps (1 Corinthians 12:28).

The gift of ministering is given to people to help the church in a supporting role. The New Testament provides examples of the gift of ministering:

Then the twelve summoned the multitude of the disciples and said, 'It is not desirable that we should leave the word of God and serve tables' (Acts 6:2).

Because there were those to help serve in supporting roles, the Twelve were able to concentrate on the work of the ministry.

And the word of God spread, and the number of the disciples multiplied greatly in Jerusalem (Acts 6:7).

The Bible speaks of others who ministered to the disciples.

So he sent into Macedonia two of those who ministered to him, Timothy and Erastus (Acts 19:22).

And when they arrived in Salamis, they preached the word of God in the synagogues of the Jews. they also had John as their assistant (Acts 13:5).

Onesimus ministered to the Apostle Paul:

I appeal to you for my son Onesimus, . . . who once was unprofitable to you, but now is profitable to you and to me (Philemon 10,11).

This appears to be another gift that all believers have been given. We all are commanded to serve God, and none who exercise this gift should be regarded as having a lesser ministry. The Apostle Paul reminded us how believers need each other.

And if they were all one member, where would the body be? But now indeed there are many members, yet one body . . . those members of the body which seem to be weaker are necessary (1 Corinthians 12:19-22).

WHAT IS THE GIFT OF SHOWING MERCY?

Showing mercy is another spiritual gift.

Having then gifts differing according to the grace that is given to us, let us use them . . . he who shows mercy with cheerfulness (Romans 12:8).

All believers are encouraged—even commanded—to show mercy.

Blessed are the merciful, for they shall obtain mercy (Matthew 5:7)

Bear one another's burdens, and so fulfill the law of Christ (Galatians 6:2).

If a brother or sister is naked and destitute of daily food, and one of you says to them, 'Depart in peace, be warmed and filled,' but you do not give them the things which are needed for the body, what does it profit (James 2:15,16).

Therefore, as we have opportunity, let us to good to all especially to those who are of the household of faith (Galatians 6:10).

The gift of showing mercy has to do with a special giving of one's time and self. It involves deeds of compassion on behalf of people in difficult situations, perhaps the sick or the down-and-out. The New Testament gives an example of the gift of showing mercy by a man named Onesiphorus. When the Apostle Paul was imprisoned in Rome, Onesiphorus showed mercy:

> The Lord grant mercy to the house of Onesiphorus, for he often refreshed me, and was not ashamed of my chain; but when he arrived in Rome, he sought me out very diligently and found me (2 Timothy 1:16,17).

Onesiphorus's example is one that every Christian should follow. He spent time and effort to help one who was having difficulty, and he continually ministered to him.

WHAT IS THE GIFT
OF MIRACLES?

The working of miracles is one of the gifts of the Spirit:

> And God has appointed these in the church; first apostles, second prophets, third teachers, after that miracles, then gifts of healing (1 Corinthians 12:28).

The gift of miracles is a supernatural, God-given ability to perform special signs that testify of God. It consists of more than the gift of healing. The Apostle Paul exercised this gift against a sorcerer who was attempting to turn away the proconsul, Sergius Paulus, from the faith.

> And now, indeed, the hand of the Lord is upon you, and you shall be blind, not seeing the sun for a time. And immediately a dark mist fell upon him, and he went around seeking someone to lead him by the hand. Then the proconsul believed, when he saw what had been done, being astonished at the teaching of the Lord (Acts 13:11).

This is a clear example of the purpose of exercising the gift of miracles. It demonstrated the power of God, through Jesus Christ, over the power of sorcery and was used to convert someone who was seeking the truth. Another example of the gift of miracles was Peter's liberation from Herod's prison (Acts 9:36-42).

Unusual Miracles

The Bible also records the Apostle Paul performing miracles.

Now God worked unusual miracles by the hands of Paul, so that even handkerchiefs or aprons were brought from his body to the sick, and the diseases left them and the evil spirits went out of them (Acts 19:11,12).

A miracle of this sort, according to the Bible, was not the norm. Why are miracles so scarce today? Any such act performed in a measurable degree would be known to the public. The fact that they are not common is due to the will of God more than the unbelief of man. It is commonly held that types of miracles are more prevalent on the mission field, where the gospel is still penetrating societies that have no knowledge of Jesus Christ. We must be careful, however, not to limit the use of miracles to the mission field.

WHAT IS THE GIFT
OF HEALING?

Scripture says that God has given gifts of healing to his church:

> To another faith by the same Spirit, to another gifts of healing by the same Spirit (1 Corinthians 12:9).

The gift is described in the plural—"gifts." Since there are different types of illness, there are different types of healing as well. The gifts of healing are not the same thing as medical knowledge or practices that help people who are sick. Rather, these gifts are supernatural abilities to restore someone to health, works that are entirely of God. "I am the Lord who heals you" (Exodus 15:26).

Peter exercised the gift of healing:

> Then Peter said, . . .'In the name of Jesus Christ of Nazareth, rise up and walk.' And he took him by the right hand and lifted him up, and immediately his feet and ankle bones received strength. So he, leaping up, stood and walked and entered the temple with them—walking, and leaping, and praising God (Acts 3:6-8).

The gift of healing is one of the sign gifts. Some believe that it was specifically for the purpose of confirming God's Word before the Bible was completed—that once the New Testament was finished the gift was withdrawn. Therefore it only had a limited use and duration. However, it is nowhere expressly stated that the gift of healing was only for a limited period of time and the burden of proof is on those who say that God no longer gives this gift.

Conform to Scripture

If indeed God is still granting the gift of healing to certain individuals, those who practice it must conform to the principles set down in Scripture. Those who exercise the gift must be judged as to their testimony for Jesus Christ. Unfortunately, there is much that goes on today under the name of divine healing that is nothing more than fraud. Some who claim to have the gift exercise it on a limited basis. There is no replacement of missing limbs, decayed teeth, hair for baldness, etc. Many of the "healings" are of the inward or psychosomatic variety.

Whenever someone claims to have the gift of healing, he should be judged according to the biblical standards and not be "blindly" followed. Moreover, one who heals with God's power will have no fear of being investigated and the healing documented.

There is also the possibility that those who are healed are healed because of something other than a supernatural work of God. The symptoms may be psychosomatic, or the healing that takes place may be a natural occurrence.

Finally, someone who genuinely has the gift of healing will draw attention to Jesus Christ and not to himself.

We may sum up concerning the gift of healing:

1. The gift of healing is the supernatural ability to restore someone to health.

2. Some believe and teach that this gift is no longer operating among believers.

3. Many who claim to have the gift of healing exercise it on a limited basis.

4. Miraculous healings may be due to something other than the faith healer.

5. Those who properly exercise the gift will do so to glorify God.

DOES GOD WANT TO
HEAL EVERYONE?

Is it God's desire that everyone who is sick be healed? If so, is there something spiritually wrong with an individual who prays for healing but remains ill?

Contrary to what some people believe and teach, the Bible clearly shows that it is not God's will to heal everybody. Scripture offers no promise that the Christian will be free from sickness in this life. The New Testament includes many such examples.

The Apostle Paul describes a "thorn in the flesh" which needed healing.

> And lest I should be exalted above measure by the abundance of revelations, a thorn in the flesh was given to me, a messenger of Satan to buffet me . . . Concerning this thing I pleaded with the Lord three times that it might depart from me. And He said to me, 'My grace is sufficient for you, for My strength is made perfect in weakness.' Therefore most gladly I will rather boast in my infirmities, that the power of Christ may rest upon me. Therefore, I take pleasure in infirmities, in reproaches, in needs, in persecutions, in distresses, for Christ's sake. For when I am weak, then I am strong (2 Corinthians 12:7-10).

Note that Paul did not assume God would heal him. He asked for healing, but was refused. God told Paul that His grace was enough. This caused the apostle to be strong in his weakness.

In another episode involving Paul, we see a similar illustration.

Erastus stayed in Corinth, but Trophimus I have left in Miletus sick (2 Timothy 4:20).

We know the Apostle Paul exercised the gift of healing. Why didn't he exercise it for Trophimus if it is God's will for everyone to be healed?

Paul told Timothy,

No longer drink only water, but use a little wine for your stomach's sake and your frequent infirmities (1 Timothy 5:23).

Timothy certainly was a man of faith, but Paul nevertheless told him to drink wine for his infirmities. The Bible says nothing of a divine right to be healed. In fact, this Scripture passage indicates that Timothy would continue at times to be sick.

Epaphroditus, on the other hand, was mercifully healed by God.

Yet I considered it necessary to send to you Epaphroditus . . . since he was longing for you all, and was distressed because you heard that he was sick. For indeed he was sick almost unto death; but God had mercy on him (Philippians 2:25-27).

Paul says that Epaphroditus was healed due to God's mercy. Epaphroditus did not invoke a certain claim to be healed.

Although God does not promise to supernaturally heal everyone, it is perfectly proper to pray that he will. The Bible says, "You do not have because you do not ask" (James 4:2).

Nowhere in the New Testament is perfect health throughout life considered the norm. Scripture never indicates that the people remained sick because they lacked faith to be healed. Neither does the Bible indicate that God heals those who "claim" or demand it. In fact, people were healed according to God's mercy. People have the right to ask God for healing, but the result is left up to Him.

WHAT ABOUT VERSES THAT
SEEM TO PROMISE HEALING?

In the New Testament, there are several instances in which Scripture seems to promise healing. One verse often cited is 1 Peter 2:24:

> Who Himself bore our sins in His own body on the tree, that we, having died to sins, might live for righteousness—by whose stripes you were healed.

With this verse many claim healing from God based upon the suffering of Christ on the cross. In context, however, this verse refers to healing from sin, not disease. It does not promise immediate healing from disease.

The healings of Jesus are used as examples to illustrate that God wishes everyone to be healed.

> When evening had come, they brought to Him many who were demon possessed. And He cast out spirits with a word, and healed all who were sick, that it might be fulfilled which was spoken by Isaiah the prophet, saying, 'He Himself took our infirmities and bore our sicknesses' (Matthew 8:16,17).

Does not the fact that Jesus healed all who were sick and had compassion upon the multitudes show us that God wants everyone well? Not at all. Jesus healed out of compassion for the people, but His healings were also a sign that He was the Messiah. He never said that it was God's desire for everyone to be made healthy.

The Bible sometimes equate sickness with sin. For those who celebrated the Lord's Supper unworthily, the Apostle Paul said,

> For this reason many are weak and sick among you, and many sleep (1 Corinthians 11:30).

But this is not always the case.

Now as Jesus passed by, He saw a man who was blind from birth. And His disciples asked Him saying, 'Rabbi, who sinned, this man or his parents, that he was born blind?' Jesus answered, 'Neither this man nor his parents sinned, but that the works of God should be revealed in him' (John 9:1-3).

God has said that He is the One who allows people to be sick. The Old Testament records God saying to Moses:

> So the Lord said to him, 'Who has made man's mouth? Or who makes the mute, the deaf, the seeing, or the blind? Have not I, the Lord?' (Exodus 4:11).

There are no Scripture verses that specifically promise healing for those who have a disease. God may have a purpose beyond our comprehension in allowing someone's sickness. Hence, we pray for His will to be done.

WHAT IS THE GIFT OF DISCERNMENT OF SPIRITS?

The Bible speaks of the gift of discernment of Spirits:

To another the working of miracles, to another prophecy, to another discerning of spirits (1 Corinthians 12:10).

Discernment of spirits is mentioned after the gift of prophecy, which provides an immediate clue as to its function. It is the ability to determine between genuine revelation from God and that which is false. When someone uttered a prophecy, it was necessary to determine whether or not that prophet was speaking from God. The Lord supernaturally gifted some individuals to determine whether the message was from Him, from that person's own imagination, or a false message from Satan. The Bible warns us of Satan's deceptions:

And no wonder! For Satan himself transforms himself into an angel of light (2 Corinthians 11:14).

The gift of discernment could also be exercised by individual believers when confronted with those bringing false doctrine.

Who is a liar but he who denies that Jesus is the Christ? He is antichrist who denies the Father and the Son. Whoever denies the Son does not have the Father either; he who acknowledges the Son has the Father also (1 John 2:22,23).

The believers were not allowed to associate with those who had accepted this false doctrine.

If anyone come to you and does not bring this doctrine, do not receive him into your house nor greet him (2 John 10).

The churches were directed to exercise the gift of discernment. The church at Ephesus is applauded for practicing the gift.

I know your works, your labor, your patience, and that you cannot bear those who are evil. And you have tested those who say they are apostles and are not, and have found them liars (Revelation 2:2).

The church at Thyatira was slack in the practice of the gift.

You allow the woman Jezebel, who calls herself a prophetess, to teach and beguile My servants to commit sexual immorality and to eat things sacrificed to idols (Revelation 2:20).

The Bible encourages believers to test the spirits.

Test all things; hold fast what is good (1 Thessalonians 5:21).

The Apostle Paul provides an example of the proper exercise of the gift.

Then Saul, who is called Paul, filled with the Holy Spirit, looked intently at him and said, 'O full of deceit and all fraud, you son of the devil, you enemy of all righteousness, will you not cease, perverting the straight ways of the Lord?' (Acts 13:9,10).

Still Available?

As with other gifts, the gift of discernment is believed by some to have been necessary only until the Bible was complete; once the New Testament was finished, the gift was no longer needed because revelation from God became complete. However, this is not indicated in the Bible. It seems more accurate to assume that God could give the same gift today to Christian leaders, to help them determine whether certain messages or teachings are from the Lord. Indeed, the gift of discerning spirits is even necessary for the church today—to test the spirits to determine if they are from God to make sure the messages are consistent with New Testament revelation.

WHAT IS THE WORD OF KNOWLEDGE?

In listing the spiritual gifts the Bible speaks about the gift of the word of knowledge.

To another the word of knowledge through the same Spirit (1 Corinthians 12:8).

The gift of the word of knowledge refers to the ability to know facts about a situation or a spiritual principle that could not have been known by natural means. This allows someone to see a situation as God sees it.

The life of Christ provides us with some examples of this ability:

Nathaniel said to Him: 'How do you know me?' Jesus answered and said to him, 'Before Philip called you, when you were under the fig tree, I saw you' (John 1:48).

When Jesus met the woman at the well, He exercised the word of knowledge:

Jesus said to her, 'Go and call your husband, and come here.' The woman answered and said, 'I have no husband.' Jesus said to her, 'You have well said, I have no husband, for you have had five husbands, and the one whom you have now is not your husband' (John 4:16-18).

Simon Peter's confession of Jesus as the Messiah was another example of this gift:

Blessed are you, Simon Bar-Jonah, for flesh and blood has not revealed this to you, but My Father who is in heaven (Matthew 16:17).

This word of knowledge is exercised when the Spirit of God provides information to someone about the condition of another person. It does not have to come with fanfare. In fact, it can be exercised without the person being aware of it. The gift must be used with a humble heart, never to take advantage of another person or situation.

The word of knowledge is not the same as the occult gifts that some spiritual mediums claim. It is not an occult power, but a God-given ability to build up the body of Christ.

WHAT IS THE
WORD OF WISDOM?

The Bible speaks of the gift of the word of wisdom. "For to one is given the word of wisdom through the Spirit" (1 Corinthians 12:8).

This is different from the gift of the word of knowledge. The word of wisdom uses knowledge for its proper end: the furtherance of God's kingdom. It can be applied in the following ways:

Through Persecution

The Holy Spirit may grant the believer the word of wisdom when answering persecutors. Jesus promised this:

> And you will be brought before governors and kings for My sake, as a testimony to them and to the Gentiles. But when they deliver you up, do not worry about how or what you should speak. For it will be given you in that hour what you should speak, for it is not you who speak, but the Spirit of your Father who speaks in you (Matthew 10:18-20).

The Book of Acts gives examples of God providing wisdom to His people under these circumstances. The gift was manifested in Peter and John as they spoke before the rulers and teachers in Jerusalem:

Now when they saw the boldness of Peter and John, and perceived that they were uneducated and untrained men, they marveled. And they realized that they had been with Jesus (Acts 4:13).

It was shown when Stephen confronted the religious leaders:

They were not able to resist the wisdom and the Spirit by which he spoke (Acts 6:10).

Defending the Faith

The word of wisdom can also be given to those defending the faith among unbelievers. We are all instructed to defend the faith:

Always be ready to give a defense to everyone who asks you a reason for the hope that is in you, with meekness and fear (1 Peter 3:15).

However, there are certain occasions when the word of wisdom is needed in answering unbeliever's questions about Christianity. Jesus exercised this many times:

Then some of the scribes answered and said, 'Teacher, You have spoke well.' But after that they dared not question Him anymore (Luke 20:39,40).

The Apostle Paul exercised this gift:

And he went into the synagogue and spoke boldly for three months, reasoning and persuading concerning the things of the kingdom of God (Acts 19:8).

Problem Solving

The word of wisdom can also be used in solving difficult problems. When the apostles were distracted from preaching the gospel because of business matters they choose certain believers to help them as administrators:

Therefore, brethren, seek out from among you seven men of good reputation, full of the Holy Spirit and wisdom whom we may appoint over business (Acts 6:3).

One of the requirements was wisdom, which was used in solving problems in the church.

Everyday Living

This gift can be used in everyday living situations. When problems arise we are told to ask for wisdom.

If any of you lacks wisdom, let him ask of God, who gives to all liberally and without reproach, and it will be given to him (James 1:5).

Thus, God will grant us wisdom on how to live a consistent life, glorifying Him.

WHAT IS THE GIFT OF TONGUES?

One of the spiritual gifts mentioned in the New Testament is the gift of tongues. Tongue-speaking, or glossolalia, is an individual's supernatural ability to speak in a language never before learned. It may be a known earthly language or an unknown heavenly language.

And God has appointed these in the church . . . varieties of tongues (1 Corinthians 12:28).

Different Purposes

The gift of tongues has three different purposes: (1) A sign to the unbeliever (2) Means to pray (3) A channel through which messages can be given to other Christians.

Sign

One of the purposes for tongues was a sign for the unbeliever:

Therefore tongues are for a sign, not to those who believe but to unbelievers (1 Corinthians 14:22).

Means of Prayer

It is a means to pray to God:

For he who who speaks in a tongue does not speak to men but to God, for no one understands him; however, in the spirit he speaks mysteries (1 Corinthians 14:2).

Channel

It is a channel through which messages are given to Christians:

For he who prophesies is greater than he who speaks with tongues, unless indeed he interprets, that the church may receive edification. But now, brethren, if I come to you speaking with tongues, what shall I profit unless I speak to you either by revelation, by knowledge, by prophesying, or by teaching? (1 Corinthians 14:5,6).

In the Book of Acts we find accounts of tongue-speaking which gave evidential value of the message of Christ (Acts 2:10).

Not Every Believer has the Gift

"Do all speak with tongues?" (1 Corinthians 12:30). The way the sentence is structured in Greek demands that the answer be no. Not everyone should be expected to speak in tongues. Furthermore, tongues is listed with all the other gifts that not every believer has.

Warnings against Misuse

The Apostle Paul spoke highly of the gift of tongues:

I wish you all spoke with tongues (1 Corinthians 14:5).

I thank my God that I speak in tongues more than you all (1 Corinthians 14:18).

But he also warned against the misuse of the gift:

But now brethren, if I come to you speaking with tongues, what shall I profit you unless I speak to you either by revelation, by knowledge, by prophesying, or by teaching? (1 Corinthians 14:6).

The Bible sets down guidelines by which the gift of tongues should be exercised. They are found in 1 Corinthians 12-14.

WHAT IS THE PROPER PROCEDURE FOR USING TONGUES IN A MEETING?

The Bible makes it clear that tongue-speaking in a Christian assembly should follow definite rules.

Build up Believers

The purpose of exercising the gift of tongues at a meeting is to build up believers, not for personal edification:

> Even so you, since you are zealous for spiritual gifts, let if be for the edification of the church that you seek to excel (1 Corinthians 14:12).

Interpreter Present

Whenever the gift is exercised in a meeting, there must be an interpreter present.

> Therefore let him who speaks in a tongue pray that he may interpret (1 Corinthians 14:13).

Limited Numbers

The Bible places a limit on the number of people allowed to speak in tongues during a meeting.

> If anyone speaks in a tongue let there be two or at the most three, each in turn, and let one interpret (1 Corinthians 14:27).

No Congregational Tongue-Speaking

The entire congregation is not supposed to speak in tongues:

> Therefore if the whole church comes together in one place, and all speak with tongues, and there comes in those who are uninformed or unbelievers, will they not say that you are out of your mind? (1 Corinthians 14:23).

Controllable

The one speaking in tongues has control over both his volume and his behavior. Any tongue speaking that is out of control is not led by God.

> And the spirit of the prophets are subjects to the prophets. For God is not the author of confusion but of peace, as in all the churches of the saints (1 Corinthians 14:32).

Even with these restrictions, though, tongue-speaking is not to be forbidden in meetings:

> Do not forbid to speak in tongues (1 Corinthians 14:39).

WERE THE TONGUES IN SCRIPTURE KNOWN LANGUAGES?

Only two portions if Scripture mention speaking in tongues: the Book of Acts and 1 Corinthians. Are the tongues referred to in these two sections known earthly languages or a heavenly language unknown to people on earth? Those who believe the tongues are always known languages do so for the following reasons:

Tongues in Acts

The first recorded episode of tongue-speaking was on the Day of Pentecost.

> And they were all filled with the Holy Spirit and began to speak with other tongues, as the Spirit gave them utterance . . . And when this sound occurred the multitude came together, and were confused, because everyone heard them speak in his own language. Then they were amazed and marveled, saying one to another, 'Look, are not all these who speak Galileans? And how is it that we hear each in our own language in which they were born? Parthians and Medes and Elamites, those dwelling in Mesopotamia, Judea and Cappadocia, Pontus and Asia, Phrygia and Pamphlia, Egypt, and parts of Libya adjoining Cyrene, visitors from Rome, both Jews and proselytes, Cretans and Arabs—we hear them speaking in our tongues the wonderful works of God' (Acts 2:4,6-11).

The tongues on this occasion were known earthly languages that the disciples had not learned. The multitude that gathered consisted of people from all over the Roman Empire. Each of them heard the disciples speak in their own particular dialect. This, of course, was a miracle, and there seems to be little doubt that the tongues were a known language.

Other occasions in the Book of Acts do not reveal whether the tongues were known earthly languages or some heavenly language. But the indication is that they were known languages. When the gospel went to the Gentiles at the house of Cornelius, Scripture indicates that the tongues were similar to those spoken on the Day of Pentecost.

For they heard them speak with tongues and magnify God (Acts 10:46).

When Peter recounted this, he added,

And as I began to speak, the Holy Spirit fell upon them, as upon us at the beginning (Acts 11:15).

"The beginning" is a reference to the Day of Pentecost. The same sign of tongues was given to the Gentiles when they believed. This may indicate that the tongues were also known languages, but of this we cannot be sure. On another occasion, Acts 19, we are not told one way or another whether the tongues were earthly languages or heavenly languages.

Prophecy of Isaiah

A prophecy in Isaiah refers to speaking with tongues:

For precept must be upon precept, line upon line. Here a little, there a little. For with stammering lips and another tongue He will speak to this people (Isaiah 28:10,11).

Isaiah predicted that the Jewish people in captivity would be spoken to in other languages. This was fulfilled with the captivities of Assyria and Babylon and the worldwide dispersion of Israel. This fulfilled a prophecy that was made earlier by Moses:

The Lord will bring a nation against you from afar, from the end of the earth, as swift as the eagle flies, a nation whose language you do not understand (Deuteronomy 28:49).

These tongues predicted by Moses were definitely foreign languages. When the Apostle Paul applied this prophecy to speaking in tongues, he implied that they also were foreign languages.

Biblical Chronology

Some people appeal to biblical chronology to solve this question. Paul's first letter to the Corinthians was written from the city of Ephesus. This letter predates the writings of Acts by approximately six years. Luke, the writer of the Book of Acts, would have been familiar with First Corinthians and with Paul's usage of the word tongues. Likewise, Luke used the word tongues. If he were aware of Paul's usage of the word to the Corinthians, then both instances are speaking of known languages.

Therefore we can sum up the situation as follows:

1. The tongues on the Day of Pentecost are most likely known languages.

2. The remainder of the instances of tongue-speaking in the Book of Acts were probably known languages.

3. The tongues in Corinthians can also be understood as known languages.

COULD TONGUE-SPEAKING BE HEAVENLY LANGUAGES RATHER THAN KNOWN LANGUAGES?

Though tongues, recorded in the Book of Acts, are most likely known earthly languages, the tongue-speaking recorded in First Corinthians seems to be a heavenly language. This is not the same as ecstatic babbling, but rather speaking in a non-earthly language. Those who believe that the tongues are sometimes heavenly languages do so for the following reasons.

While Acts 2 strongly implies that the tongue-speaking was in known languages, the other instances in the Book of Acts do not. The sign of tongues, not the tongue language, is what convinced Peter that the Gentiles believed in Christ. There is no indication that anyone understood the languages that Cornelius and his group spoke when they received the Holy Spirit.

But even if the tongues in Acts all were known languages, those recorded in First Corinthians seem to be of a different sort. In Acts, the tongue-speaking occurred in a situation where people received the initial indwelling of the Holy Spirit. When Paul discusses tongues in First Corinthians, his concern is the worship service. In addition, there are several remarks made by the Apostle Paul which indicates the tongues were heavenly languages:

Though I speak with the tongues of men and of angels (1 Corinthians 13:1).

For he who speaks in a tongue does not speak to men but to God, for no one understands him; however, in the spirit he speaks mysteries (1 Corinthians 14:2).

For if I pray in a tongue, my spirit prays, but my understanding is unfruitful (1 Corinthians 14:4).

All these verses seem to refer to a heavenly language.

Arguments Against this View

Those who believe that the tongue-speaking in both cases refers to known languages respond to these verses in the following manner:

1. Though the situation in Acts and Corinthians are different, the tongues are still the same. Since the first instance of tongue-speaking in Acts refers to known languages, one could assume that known languages were spoken in the other instances as well.

2. When Paul mentions speaking in the tongues of angels (1 Corinthians 13:1), he probably meant it theoretically.

3. First Corinthians 14:2 refers to the general audience as not understanding the uttered language, and has nothing to do with a heavenly language.

4. First Corinthians 14:14 refers to the one praying in a language which he does not understand, which may be only a foreign language.

These responses, however, are not necessarily convincing, and when the evidence is weighed either view can be supported.

IF CERTAIN TONGUE SPEAKING DOES NOT COME FROM GOD, WHERE DOES IT COME FROM?

Some say that if tongue-speaking does not come from God, the source must be Satan. It is possible that some tongue-speaking may originate from Satan. Jesus referred to him as the father of lies:

> He was a murderer from the beginning, and does not stand in the truth, because there is no truth in him. When he speaks a lie, he speaks from his own resources, for he is a liar and the father of it (John 8:44).

However, there can be tongue-speaking that originates from the speaker's human nature. Someone, with the best of intentions, can speak out believing that he is speaking in tongues. If his utterance is not a gift from God, we do not need to attribute it to the devil, but rather to his own exuberance.

When speaking in tongues is exercised in a congregation there are basically four possibilities to its origin:

1. The tongue is an unknown language to the speaker but known to someone in the congregation.

2. The tongue is a known language in heaven but unknown to anyone on earth. In this case someone must give an interpretation.

3. The tongue is a nonrational ecstatic utterance that originates from the mind of the speaker.

4. The tongue-speaking is demonic and comes from a counterfeit spirit.

Whenever tongue-speaking is exercised, the believers are encouraged to test the spirits:

> Beloved, do not believe every spirit, but test the spirits, whether they are of God; because many false prophets are gone out into the world (1 John 4:1).

WHAT IS THE GIFT OF INTERPRETATION OF TONGUES?

When tongues are used in a worship service, according to Scripture the uttered message is to be interpreted. This is accomplished by those who have the gift of interpretation of tongues. The Bible says the interpretation of tongues is a spiritual gift (1 Corinthians 12:10).

The interpreter turns the attention of the congregation for the one speaking toward God. The Apostle Paul insisted that every time the gift of tongues was exercised publicly, it should be interpreted:

> If anyone speaks in a tongue, let there be two or at the most three, each in turn, and let one interpret. But if there is no interpreter, let him keep silent in the church, and let him speak to himself and to God (1 Corinthians 14:13).

The gift of interpretation of tongues is as supernatural ability to understand the tongue language and translate it. It is not the ability to translate a foreign language.

WHAT ARGUMENTS HAVE BEEN GIVEN FOR THE CESSATION OF THE SIGN GIFTS?

There has been considerable controversy over whether or not some of the so-called gifts as recorded in the New Testament still exist in the church. These sign gifts, which include apostleship, prophecy, healing, miracles, speaking in tongues, and the interpretation of tongues, are said to have ceased with the death of the apostles.

Confirm the Word

These gifts as the argument goes, were temporary; to help establish the church and to confirm the Word before written revelation—the Bible—was complete. These signs also were given to authenticate the gospel message. Once the Bible was finished, there was no more need for these miraculous gifts. This being the case, anyone who exercises these gifts today is not doing it by the power of God.

Still Available?

Are these gifts still to be used by the church or has God withdrawn them? The main arguments for the cessation of spiritual gifts can be broken down into six basic categories. They include:

1. THE PURPOSE OF THE GIFTS

2. THE PLAN OF GOD IN HISTORY

3. THE EVIDENCE FROM THE NEW TESTAMENT

4. EVIDENCE FROM THE BOOK OF ACTS

5. CHURCH HISTORY

6. EXPERIENCE

We will examine each of these arguments individually and then give a response to the arguments.

DOES THE PURPOSE OF THE SIGN GIFTS INDICATE THEY HAVE CEASED?

There are those that argue that the very purpose of the sign gifts are a clear indication that they were meant to be temporary and have now ceased. They say the purpose of the sign gifts was to confirm the Word of God in a special way. They were foundational gifts to the church. Before the New Testament had been committed to writing, these signs served as confirmation of God's Word. Once the New Testament was completed, the sign gifts were no longer necessary. Upon the death of the apostles, these miraculous gifts ceased.

One of the arguments used is the gift of apostleship.

Therefore, of these men who have accompanied us all the time that the Lord Jesus went in and out among us, beginning from the baptism of John to that day when He was taken up from us, one of these must become a witness with us of His resurrection (Acts 1:22,23).

Since nobody today can fill these qualifications, the gift has supposedly ceased.

Sign to Israel

It is also argued that tongues were only a sign to Israel. If God stopped dealing with Israel in A.D. 70, as some argue, then the gift is no longer necessary. If the purpose of the sign gifts were to confirm the Word before the New Testament was completed, then they are no longer for today.

Response

The confirmation of the Word was one of the purposes of the sign gifts—but that does not mean it was the only purpose. The miracles were more than just signs. The raising of Dorcas (Acts 9:36-42) may have been for the purpose of restoring a key purpose to the community rather than as a sign to confirm the Word.

In addition, the sign gifts were not limited to the apostles. Others exhibited miraculous gifts.

> And Stephen, full of faith and power, did great wonders and signs among the people (Acts 6:8).

Furthermore, we may ask the question as to why the sign gifts were given to the church at Corinth where no apostle lived? We know that the ministry of healing was to be an ongoing ministry in the church.

> Is anyone among you sick? Let him call for the elders of the church, and let them pray over him, anointing him with oil in the name of the Lord. And the prayer of faith will save the sick, and the Lord will raise him up (James 5:14,15).

Some accuse the practitioners of prophecy of adding to God's Word. This is not accurate, however. Those who argue this define prophecy in a very narrow sense, apart from its biblical meaning and purpose. Prophecy is not only adding new revelation but can include other things:

> But he who prophesies speaks edification and exhortation and comfort to men (1 Corinthians 14:3).

Most important, the sign gifts are never listed separate from the other gifts. The Bible never classifies them differently. Furthermore, the Bible does not make a distinction between temporary gifts and those that will last during the entire church age. Therefore the argument for cessation of the sign gifts from their purpose is not very strong.

DOES EVIDENCE FROM THE PLAN OF GOD INDICATE THE SIGN GIFTS HAVE CEASED?

Some people say that the sign gifts have now ceased because they no longer play a part in the plan of God. The argument reasons that miraculous signs have only appeared during new periods of revelation to confirm the Word of God.

When the program of God is examined from the pages of the Bible, one can find only three periods of history when God worked miraculous signs. One was during the time of Moses. Exodus 1-11 indicates that the purpose of these miraculous signs, done through Moses, was to authenticate the Word of God before Pharaoh. When the Israelites entered the Promised Land, the miracles died out.

The other examples were of the lives of Elijah and Elisha. They were sent to confirm God's Word to a sinful nation. When they died, the miracles died with them.

God worked during other Old Testament times without having to display any supernatural miracles to confirm His Word. During the time of Ezra and Nehemiah, for example, God was working His program without the confirmation from miraculous signs. Therefore, it is not necessary that the miraculous signs exist for God to perform His program.

The miracles appeared in clusters only two different times in the Old Testament: the time of the Exodus, and the ministry of Elijah and Elisha. The ministry of Jesus and the apostles represented the third and final cluster of miracles. Each cluster of miracles occurred for a specific purpose: to authenticate God's Word. Now that the Bible is complete, no further authentication is necessary. Hence the purpose of the miracles in the plan of God demonstrates they are no longer needed.

Response

The argument for the cessation of the gifts from the purpose and plan of God is not convincing for several reasons. First, other miracles occurred besides the ones during the so-called confirmation periods. Scripture is full of examples of God performing miraculous deeds in the lives of believers, including Gideon, Samson, Daniel, Jonah, and Joshua. To argue, as some do, that they are found only in clusters is not accurate.

In addition, it is difficult to put the miracles of Elijah and Elisha in the category of confirming signs. There was no new revelation when they performed their miracles. There was no written Scripture to confirm. The period in which they lived was no more pivotal than the time of Jeremiah and the destruction of Jerusalem. To say that the cluster of miracles happened during their time to confirm a new period of revelation lacks biblical support.

Most of the so-called confirming miracles at the time of Elijah and Elisha were done in private, out of view of most of the nation (1 Kings 17:22-23; 2 Kings 2:11-14, 19-22; 4:32-37; 5:14; 6:5-7; 13:21). It is difficult to understand how these can be considered as confirming new revelation when they were not done in public.

Even if it were true that the miracles only came in two clusters during the Old Testament period, it still does not mean that this would necessarily be the case in the New Testament.

Therefore the argument from the plan of God for the cessation of the sign gifts is not convincing.

DOES THE NEW TESTAMENT TEACH THAT THE SIGN GIFTS HAVE CEASED?

Those who argue for the cessation of the sign gifts at the end of the first century appeal to the evidence of the New Testament writers to back up their claim.

First Corinthians 13:8-10

> Love never fails. But whether there are prophecies, they will fail, whether there are tongues, they will cease; whether there is knowledge, it will vanish away. For we know in part and prophesy in part. But when that which is perfect has come, then that which is in part will be done away.

These verses teach that prophecy, tongues, and knowledge will someday cease. The question is: When will this occur? Those who believe the sign gifts are not for today argue that they ceased of themselves at the end of the apostolic period.

The word translated cease is the Greek word *katargeo*, which in this context means "cease of itself." The gift of tongues, the argument goes, ceased of itself when the apostles died. The sign gifts were given to authenticate the gospel until the Bible was completed. Once the Scripture had been completed, there was no more need for signs because the Word of God was then perfect and available.

The question comes up about the meaning of *perfect*. What does it refer to. Some people believe that *perfect* refers to the Bible. When it was completed there was no more need for signs. The words *to telion*, translated "the perfect," are in the neuter gender. This leads some to believe it cannot refer to Christ.

Response

Tongues will indeed "cease of themselves," but only when the "perfect" has come. "Perfect" refers to the perfect age when Christ returns.

> Beloved, now are we children of God; and it has not yet been revealed what we shall be, but we know when He is revealed, we shall be like Him, for we shall see Him as He is (1 John 3:2).

The idea that Paul had in his mind a completed Scripture when referring to "perfect" is highly unlikely. Many of those who reject the sign gifts realize that this argument does not carry much weight.

The reference to prophecies, knowledge, and miracles are not meant to indicate their temporary nature during the period of the church age. There will be no need for them only when Christ returns.

Hebrew 2:4

> God also bearing witness both with signs and wonders, with various miracles, and gifts of the Holy Spirit, according to His own will.

Those who heard the Lord were the apostles. How was someone to know whether or not the message of the apostles was to be trusted? By "signs and wonders." This verse says that God had (past tense) born witness to His Word by means of the sign gifts. When this letter was written to the Hebrews, the signs had already died out.

Response

If the sign gifts were given to confirm apostolic authority, then why did non-apostles have the sign gifts?

> And Stephen, full of faith and power, did great wonders and signs among the people (Acts 6:8).

And the multitudes with one accord heeded the things spoken by Philip, hearing and seeing the miracles which he did (Acts 8:6).

Furthermore, why were the sign gifts given at the church of Corinth, where no apostle lived? This verse says that the signs had been performed among the unbelievers. It does not say that they ceased or that they were limited to the first generation of believers.

Ephesians 2:20

Having been built on the foundation of the apostles and prophets, Jesus Christ Himself being the chief cornerstone.

This verse is said by some to mean that the gifts, manifested through the apostles and prophets, were foundational to the church. Once the foundation had been built, however, there was no need to build upon this foundation. In addition, some argue that once the job was finished, there was no further need for the offices of apostle and prophet.

Response

There are many assumptions that one must make to come to this conclusion, but none are supported by Scripture. It must be assumed that the apostles and prophets had only a temporary purpose, and this purpose was the confirmation of God's Word. It also must be assumed that the gifts functioned with them and no one else. Both of these arguments lack support.

Revelation 22:18

For I testify to everyone who hears the word of the prophecy of this book: If anyone adds to these things God will add to him the plagues that are written in this book.

Once the Bible was completed, there is no more need for the sign gifts, because nothing needs to be added to Scripture.

Response

If this were taken literally, then the only book of the Bible could be believed is the Book of Revelation! The verse cited says not to add or take away from the prophecies of this book—Revelation. Thus, it would have to be the only book you could believe. To make this refer to the entire Bible is highly speculative. Furthermore sign gifts do not add to Scripture. They merely apply, interpret, witness and confirm Scripture.

Lack of Mention in New Testament Letters

Another argument for the cessation of the sign gifts concerns their lack of mention. The letter to the Corinthian church is the only place sign gifts are mentioned. The list of spiritual gifts in the letter to the Romans (Romans 12:3-8) and the letter to the Ephesians (Ephesians 4:11-13) does mention the sign gifts. If they were permanent gifts, then the other letters would have mentioned them.

Response

This is an argument from silence. The Scripture nowhere makes a distinction between the sign gifts and the other gifts. If the sign gifts as tongues were to soon cease, why did the Apostle Paul write to the Corinthians: "Do not forbid to speak with tongues" (1 Corinthians 14:39)?

Therefore, the New Testament does not give evidence that the sign gifts have ceased.

DOES THE BOOK OF ACTS PROVIDE EVIDENCE THAT THE SIGN GIFTS HAVE CEASED?

Some have argued that the Book of Acts gives proof that the sign gifts were not necessary beyond the first century. The Book of Acts reveals that the Old Testament Scriptures did not have to be authenticated by signs; they were the final court of appeal.

> For Moses truly said to the fathers, 'The Lord your God will raise for you a Prophet like me from your brethren. Him you shall hear in all things, whatever He says to you.' And it shall come to pass that every soul who will not hear the Prophet shall be utterly destroyed from among the people.' Yes, and all the prophets, from Samuel and those who follow, as many as have been spoken, have also foretold these days (Acts 3:22-24).

Whenever the Old Testament was cited, it was believed and did not have to be confirmed. This means that once the Word of God had been committed to writing, there was no longer any need for authentication. Thus, the New Testament Scriptures also should be believed without external confirmation. Since the miraculous gifts appear on the scene only during periods of prophecy or new revelation, they are no longer necessary. With the completion of the New Testament we see the cessation of the miraculous gifts.

Response

The argument for the cessation of the gifts from the Book of Acts is also not conclusive. Again, those who argue this way assume what they should be proving. To assume that the gifts were the confirmation of the Word of God and had no other purpose does not fit the facts. The description of the use of certain of the gifts in 1 Corinthians 12-14 shows that they had a purpose beyond confirming the Word.

Miraculous signs did not appear only during times of new revelation for confirmational purposes of the written Word. Many examples can be cited where God performed miracles without adding new revelation.

Why, it may be asked, would certain gifts become unnecessary when the Word was committed to writing? Is there something about the written Word that makes it more believable than the spoken word?

Thus, the argument from the Book of Acts is inconclusive.

DOES HISTORY GIVE EVIDENCE OF SIGN GIFTS HAVING CEASED?

One of the most-often voiced objections to the modern-day usage of the sign gifts is an argument from history. The cessationists argue that once the apostles died those sign gifts died with them. The following historical arguments are given against the sign gifts continuing in the church:

1. There is no evidence that the sign gifts survived the apostles. The testimony of church history is that the sign gifts ceased with the death of the apostles. The second generation of Christians did not practice the gift.

2. Some early church leaders plainly asserted that the gifts were no longer practiced in their time. Early church leaders such as John Chrysostom, Theodore, and Augustine said the sign gifts were not being exercised in the church.

3. Those who did practice the gifts were from heretical or cultic groups. Any exercise of the sign gifts was by fringe groups. The mainline church did not exercise the sign gifts.

4. The church has never officially emphasized and substantiated the use of the gifts. They have been absent from the church throughout its history.

Response

The information we have is incomplete with regard to early Christianity, but there is plenty of evidence that the sign gifts did not die out with the apostles.

Iranaeus (A.D. 130-200) described spiritual gifts in his day:

> Others have foreknowledge of things to come: they see visions, and utter prophetic expressions. Others still, heal the sick by laying their hands of them, and they are made whole (Philip Schaff, Iranaeus Against Heresies Ante-Nicene: 100-325, vol. 2 of the *The History of the Christian Church*, Grand Rapids: Eerdmans, 1973, p. 531).

In A.D. 257 Novation wrote:

> This is He who places the prophets in the Church, instructs teachers, directs tongues, gives powers and healings, does wonderful works, offers discrimination of spirits, affords powers of government, suggest counsels, and orders and arranges whatever other gifts, there are of charismata; and thus makes the Lord's church everywhere, and in all, perfected, and completed (Philip Schaff, "Treatise Concerning the Trinity, XXIX," Ante-Nicene: 100-325, vol. 2 of *The History of the Christian Church*, Grand Rapids, Eerdmans, 1973, p. 641).

There are other early references to the existence and exercise of the gifts by Tertullian (A.D. 160-200) and Bishop Hillary who died in A.D. 367. Thus the idea that spiritual gifts immediately ceased with the apostles is untrue. The sign gifts remained and were exercised to varying degrees in the early church.

It is true that some church leaders spoke out against the exercise of the sign gifts. But one of them, St. Augustine, changed his mind later in life. He wrote:

> But what I said is not to be interpreted that no miracles are believed to be performed in the name of Christ at the present time. For when I wrote that book, I myself had recently learned that a blind man had been restored to sight . . . and I known about some others, so numerous even in these times, that we cannot know about all of them or enumerate those who know.

Those who practiced the supernatural gifts during this period are unfairly singled out as extremists and heretics. Iranaeus, Justin, and Augustine, who cite their continued use in the early centuries, are respected church leaders, not cultists.

No theology of spiritual gifts developed in the church until recently. John Wesley, the founder of the Methodist church, believed the gifts fell out of use because the spiritual state of the people. He wrote:

> The cause of their decline was not as has been vulgarly supposed because there was no need for them, because all the world were become Christians . . . the real cause was: the love of many, almost all Christians so called was waxed cold . . . this was the real cause why the extraordinary gifts of the Holy Spirit were no longer to be found in the Christian church; because the Christians were turned heathen again and had only a dead form left (cited by Michael Harper, *As at the Beginning: The Twentieth Century Pentecostal Revival*, Plainfield, New Jersey: Logos International, 1971, pp. 17,18).

Spiritual gifts were not given much attention in the church until recently. Therefore the lack of their mention should not cause us to draw any premature conclusions.

We may conclude, therefore, by saying that the testimony of church history shows that the gifts did not cease immediately with the apostles but were used by others after them.

WHAT DOES EXPERIENCE SAY ABOUT THE PERMANENCE OF THE SIGN GIFTS?

The last and most frequent argument mentioned against the sign gifts is experience. Does experience show us that the miraculous gifts no longer function in the church?

The following contentions are often raised:

Why Are They Not Visible?

If the sign gifts still exist, why do we not see them being exercised? Why are there no miraculous healings, people being raised from the dead, or the blind receiving sight? If the sign gifts are indeed being exercised, we should expect to see them used.

Sign Gifts Cause Division

Some people argue that the divisive nature of the gifts demonstrates that they are not from God. Many times when people come into a church and exercise sign gifts they cause divisions within that group. Dividing the body of Christ is not the work of the Holy Spirit. Thus, it is argued that those who exercise the sign gifts show a lack of spiritual maturity.

Response

The miraculous sign gifts may not occur frequently, but God can still produce them if He so desires. The situation as recorded in the Book of Acts is that miracles were the exception to the rule, they were not happening everywhere with every believer.

Without a doubt spiritual gifts are overemphasized by some charismatic Christians, but their misuse or abuse of spiritual gifts has nothing to do with their authenticity. The practice of spiritual gifts does not belong exclusively to immature, ignorant, believers. It is unfair to place all those who practice the sign gifts in this category. Nor do they always cause division within the groups where they operate.

The argument from experience proves nothing, for many would testify that their experience teaches them that the sign gifts are still with the church. Experience does not determine doctrine. We should not conform our doctrine to our experience, but we should conform experience to doctrine. The issue is not what we have personally experienced but rather what the Bible says.

WHY IS THERE SO MUCH DIVISION OVER SPIRITUAL GIFTS?

The subject of spiritual gifts causes much division among believers. This is extremely unfortunate, because one of the ministries of the Holy Spirit is to unify the believers in Christ. Paul wrote to the Ephesians,

> Endeavoring to keep the unity of the Spirit in the bond of peace (Ephesians 4:3).

Fear of Unknown

It is acceptable that people hold different views upon the subject of spiritual gifts, but it is wrong when the differences cause division. One of the reasons for the division over spiritual gifts is ignorance. When something new or unusual occurs in the church, people may naturally experience fear. Many people have their own particular view of what God will and will not do, and may not be open to differing points of view.

Tradition

Another cause for the divisions over spiritual gifts is tradition. The Bible scholar F.F. Bruce provides an example of how tradition can color one's view of a subject:

A group of biblicist churches in a certain country was under the influence of a few Pentecostal teachers. Their leaders were particularly concerned at the increasing practice of glossolalia (speaking in tongues) which was attributed to the influence of Pentecostal visitors. It might have been thought that, since glossolalia was a feature of some apostolic churches, it would have been acceptable in a biblicist community—but it was not countenanced in the tradition of these churches. There were historical reasons for this, arising from the differences between their spiritual ancestors and Edward Irving, but they were probably unaware of this. They would not have wished to appeal to tradition: Scripture was their authority. But while Scripture discourages an over-high evaluation of glossolalia, it does not forbid the due exercise of the gift. The leaders of the affected churches, however, inherited an interpretation of 1 Corinthians 13:10, 'When the perfect comes, the imperfect will pass away,' which took it to mean that glossolalia and similar manifestations of the Spirit were intended to be temporary, and would pass away when the New Testament canon was complete. In one circular letter that they issued on the subject, they appealed to this as the 'standard' interpretation in their churches. Quite apart from the validity of the exegesis—and that the concept of the completed New Testament canon was present to Paul's mind is extremely improbable (F.F. Bruce, *Tradition: Old and New,* Grand Rapids, Zondervan, 1971, p. 14).

Differences of opinion over spiritual gifts are acceptable—unless they cause division.

CONCLUSION TO PART 3

After surveying what the Bible says concerning spiritual gifts we conclude the following:

1. Spiritual gifts are God-given enablements to the believer for the purpose of service.

2. Every believer has a spiritual gift.

3. Believers are encouraged to exercise their spiritual gifts.

4. The purpose of the gifts are for the profit of the body of Christ.

5. The Bible lists about twenty spiritual gifts. There may be others.

6. Some believe that certain miraculous gifts, known as sign gifts, are no longer given by God.

7. The evidence that the sign gifts have ceased is not convincing.

8. Certain of the supernatural gifts, such as speaking in tongues, are abused. Yet this does not mean they should be neglected.

9. Different opinions about spiritual gifts are acceptable unless they cause division.

PART 4

THE HOLY SPIRIT AND
THE INDIVIDUAL

WHAT DOES IT MEAN TO BE "BORN OF THE SPIRIT?"

The Scriptures speak of the necessity of being "born of the Spirit." Jesus said,

> Most assuredly, I say to you, unless one is born of water and the Spirit, he cannot enter the kingdom of God (John 3:5).

Being "born of the Spirit" is also referred to as the "new birth." The new birth is the work of the Holy Spirit, who places the believer in a right relationship with God. It is a work of God, not of man:

> Who were born, not of blood, nor of the will of flesh, nor of the will of man, but of God (John 1:13).

Necessity

The new birth is necessary because all of us have been separated from God because of our sin.

> For all have sinned and fall short of the glory of God (Romans 3:23).

If we continue in our sin there is no hope for us. "For the wages of sin is death" (Romans 6:23).

Yet if we trust Christ as Savior, salvation can be ours.

But the gift of God is eternal life in Christ Jesus our Lord (Romans 6:23).

The new birth occurs when faith is placed in Christ:

But as many as received Him, to them He gave the right to become children of God, even to those who believe in His name (John 1:12).

This regenerating work of the Holy Spirit is necessary for everyone.

Not by works of righteousness which we have done, but according to His mercy He saved us, through the washing of regeneration and renewing of the Holy Spirit (Titus 3:5).

The new birth is an act of God. This experience is accomplished by placing faith in Christ as Savior.

WHAT IS THE INDWELLING
OF THE HOLY SPIRIT?

One of the ministries of the Holy Spirit is His indwelling. The Bible teaches that the Holy Spirit indwells all who believe in Christ. The gospel of John records Jesus saying:

> On the last day, that great day of the feast, Jesus stood and cried out saying, 'If anyone thirsts, let him come to Me and drink. He who believes in Me, as the Scripture has said, out of his heart will flow rivers of living water.' But this He spoke concerning the Spirit, whom those believing in Him would receive; for the Holy Spirit was not yet given, because Jesus was not yet glorified (John 7:37-39).

The Apostle John wrote:

> No one has seen God at any time. If we love one another, God abides in us, and His love has been perfected in us. By this we know that we abide in Him, and He in us, because He has given us of His Spirit. And we have seen and testify that the Father has sent the Son as Savior of the world (1 John 4:12-14).

The indwelling of the Holy Spirit occurs the moment a person receives Christ as Savior. The Spirit then begins His work in the life of the believer.

What does this mean to the individual? The indwelling ministry of the Holy Spirit allows Christ to dwell in our hearts forever. God can now work in a believer's life, helping that person conform to the character of God.

For whom He foreknew, He also predestined to be conformed to the image of His Son, that He might be the firstborn among many brethren (Romans 8:29).

The indwelling work of the Spirit also gives the believer the security of knowing he is a child of God:

In whom also, having believed, you were sealed with the Holy Spirit of promise (Ephesians 1:13).

WHEN DOES A PERSON RECEIVE THE HOLY SPIRIT?

When does a person receive the Holy Spirit into his life? The New Testament teaches that the reception of the Holy Spirit is something that takes place immediately upon believing in Christ as Savior. There is no need to wait or plead for the Holy Spirit. All those who believe in Jesus instantaneously receive the Holy Spirit. This the Scripture makes clear.

The Apostle Paul wrote to the Galatians:

Did you receive the Spirit by the works of the law, or by the hearing of faith? (Galatians 3:2).

And because you are sons, God has sent forth the Spirit of His Son into your hearts (Galatians 4:6).

The Bible says that a person could not be a believer without the Holy Spirit:

But you are not in the flesh but in the Spirit, if indeed the Spirit of God dwells in you. Now if anyone does not have the Spirit of Christ, he is not His (Romans 8:9).

These are sensual persons, who cause divisions, not having the Spirit (Jude 19).

Furthermore, all Christians, no matter what their spiritual condition, are said to have the Holy Spirit. The Apostle Paul wrote to the church at Corinth:

Do you not know that you are the temple of God and
that the Spirit of God dwells in you (1 Corinthians 3:16).

The church at Corinth had many spiritual problems,
yet the Apostle Paul said every believer, those walking in
the Spirit and those who were not, had received the Holy
Spirit.

In addition, there is no command to seek for the Holy
Spirit or to pray so He can be received. If the Holy Spirit
were given apart from salvation, we would expect the Bible
to give the requirements of His reception.

Gift to All Who Believe

The Holy Spirit is a gift to all who believe.

Now hope does not disappoint, because the love of God
has been poured out in our hearts by the Holy Spirit who
was given to us (Romans 5:5).

Now we have received, not the spirit of the world, but
the Spirit who is from God, that we may know the things
that have been freely given to us by God (1 Corinthians
2:12).

Therefore, we can conclude that a person receives the
Holy Spirit upon believing for the following reasons:

1   The Bible expressly says so.

2   Those without the Holy Spirit are considered
    unbelievers.

3   All believers are spoken to as though they had the Holy
    Spirit.

4   Nowhere is the believer encouraged to pray and receive
    the Holy Spirit.

5   The Holy Spirit is a gift, not a reward for faith or service

ARE THERE OUTWARD SIGNS OF RECEIVING THE HOLY SPIRIT?

The Holy Spirit is received when a person believes in Jesus Christ. Should we expect some outward sign that the Holy Spirit has been received? Although certain individuals in the New Testament exhibited signs when they received the Holy Spirit, such as speaking in tongues, the Bible does not allow us to make this the norm for everyone.

On the Day of Pentecost the disciples of Jesus received the gift of tongues when the Holy Spirit came upon them:

And they were all filled with the Holy Spirit and began to speak with other tongues, as the Spirit gave them utterance (Acts 2:4).

When Peter then preached to the multitude, he promised them the Holy Spirit upon believing:

Then Peter said to them, 'Repent, and let every one of you be baptized in the name of the Jesus Christ for the remission of sins; and you shall receive the gift of the Holy Spirit' (Acts 2:38).

Yet, when these people believed, there is no indication of any outward signs of their reception of the Holy Spirit:

Then those who gladly received his word were baptized; and that day about three thousand souls were added to them (Acts 2:41).

As we study different accounts of conversion as recorded in the Book of Acts we find no accompanying signs in the following instances: 4:4; 6:7; 8:14-36; 9:1-42; 17:32-34.

In writing to the Corinthians the Apostle Paul asked, "Do all speak with tongues?" (1 Corinthians 12:30). The question is asked in such a way that the Greek grammar demands an answer of no. If tongues were a sign of receiving the Holy Spirit, then Paul would have not asked the question.

The evidence of the reception of the Holy Spirit is not so much an outward sign but a changed life:

> Therefore, if anyone is in Christ, he is a new creation; old things have passed away; behold all things have become new (2 Corinthians 5:17).

Therefore, rather than expecting some outward evidence of receiving the Holy Spirit, we should expect to see changes in our lives. This is the evidence a person has received the Holy Spirit.

CAN A PERSON LOSE
THE HOLY SPIRIT?

Once the Holy Spirit enters a person, can He leave? In Psalm 51, David prayed,

Do not cast me away from Your presence, and do not take Your Holy Spirit from me (Psalm 51:11).

The Bible gives the example of the Holy Spirit leaving Samson:

And she said, 'The Philistines are upon you, Samson!' So he awoke, from his sleep, and said, 'I will go out as before, at other times, and shake myself free!' But he did not know that the Lord had departed from him (Judges 16:20).

In another instance, the Holy Spirit is said to have left Saul:

But the Spirit of the Lord departed from Saul, and a distressing spirit from the Lord troubled him (1 Samuel 16:14).

These passages seem to teach that one can lose the Holy Spirit. But this is not necessarily the case. There are other possible solutions to this question. Some believe that the situations of David, Samson, and Saul must be understood in their Old Testament context. It appears that during that period, the Holy Spirit did not indwell believers on a permanent basis; but rather His presence in the life of the believer was of a limited duration.

Special Anointing

A second view holds that it was not the indwelling of the Holy Spirit that left these people, but a particular anointing or empowering of the Spirit that departed. David and Saul were kings and had a special anointing from God to rule the people. Samson also had a special anointing from God to lead Israel. What left Samson and Saul and what David prayed to retain was not the indwelling of the Holy Spirit but rather the Holy Spirit's anointing to rule. In the same way, the Holy Spirit always indwells a believer, but can anoint that New Testament believer for a specific and temporary purpose.

Whatever the case may be, the New Testament makes it plain that the Holy Spirit will not leave the believer.

And I will pray the Father, and He will give you another Helper, that He may abide with you forever (John 14:16).

Having believed, you were sealed with the Holy Spirit of promise, who is the guarantee of our inheritance until the redemption of the purchased possession (Ephesians 1:13,14).

HOW DOES THE HOLY SPIRIT 'SEAL' THE BELIEVER?

When a person receives Christ as Savior, the Bible says that the Holy Spirit seals, or guarantees, that the individual is a child of God. It confirms the fact that the Holy Spirit will never leave him. The Scripture says:

Who also has sealed us and given us the Spirit in our hearts as a deposit (2 Corinthians 1:22).

In Him you also trusted, after you heard the word of truth, the gospel of your salvation; in whom also, having believed, you were sealed with the Holy Spirit of promise (Ephesians 1:13).

And do not grieve the Holy Spirit of God, by whom you were sealed for the day of redemption (Ephesians 4:30).

From these passages we can deduce the following concerning the sealing of the Holy Spirit:

1. All believers are sealed by the Holy Spirit. The church in Corinth included believers who were spiritually immature and had gross sin in their lives. Yet they were all sealed with the Spirit. Furthermore, the Scriptures nowhere command the believer to be sealed with the Spirit. All believers are assumed to be sealed.

2. The sealing takes place the moment a person trusts Christ as Savior.

3. The sealing of the Holy Spirit is a non-experiential ministry of the Spirit. It takes place without the believer directly experiencing it.

4. When the Holy Spirit seals the believer, He guarantees that person's security. The sealing is a promise that the salvation the Christian receives is granted both now and forever.

WHAT IS THE ANOINTING OF THE HOLY SPIRIT?

The Apostle John told his readers that they had been anointed with the Holy Spirit.

But you have an anointing from the Holy One, and you know all things. . . But the anointing which you have received from Him abides in you, and you do not need that anyone teach you; but as the same anointing teaches you concerning all things, and is true, and is not a lie, and just as it has taught you, you will abide in Him (1 John 2:20,27).

The only other reference in the New Testament to the anointing of the Spirit was by the Apostle Paul.

Now He who establishes us with you in Christ has anointed us is God (2 Corinthians 1:21).

From these verses we conclude that it is God who anoints the believer with the Spirit. This "anointing" remains forever with the believer. The purpose of this anointing is that the believer might be taught.

HOW DOES A PERSON BECOME FILLED WITH THE HOLY SPIRIT?

The Bible commands the believer to be filled with the Holy Spirit.

> And do not be drunk with wine, in which is dissipation; but be filled with the Spirit (Ephesians 5:18).

> I say then: Walk in the Spirit, and you shall not fulfill the lust of the flesh (Galatians 5:16).

The Bible does not give any set formula for being filled with the Holy Spirit. There is not a series of stages which a person must go through. Nor is there a need to wait for the filling of the Spirit. The filling is available to every believer.

Some have felt the need to wait or tarry for the Holy Spirit based upon a statement of Jesus:

> Behold, I send the Promise of My Father upon you; but tarry in the city of Jerusalem until you are endued with power from on high (Luke 24:49).

But this statement of Jesus was directed at His disciples. They were told to wait in Jerusalem until the Day of Pentecost, when the Holy Spirit would descend in a permanent way upon all believers. This was a once-and-for-all occurrence. Once this had happened, there was no need to wait to be filled with the Spirit.

How, then, does a person become filled with the Spirit? He must obey the things God has commanded of Him in the Bible. The key to being controlled by the Holy Spirit is obedience.

The Bible instructs the believer to seek to please God. When he turns his life over to God he places himself in a position to be controlled by the Holy Spirit. The believer then can find out what God requires of him by studying His Word. Once he understands what God wants him to do he can be filled with the Spirit by obeying God's commandments. When we sin, the fellowship between God and us is broken. We need to confess our sins and yield to Him so we may again be filled with the Spirit.

If we confess our sins, He is faithful and just to forgive us our sins and to cleanse us from all unrighteousness (1 John 1:9).

WHAT ARE THE RESULTS OF BEING FILLED WITH THE SPIRIT?

Once a person is filled with the Holy Spirit, what are the results in a person's life?

One of the results of allowing the continual filling of the Holy Spirit is spiritual maturity. This has visible results known as the fruit of the Spirit.

Fruit of the Spirit

But the fruit of the Spirit is love, joy peace, longsuffering, kindness, goodness, faithfulness, gentleness, self-control. Against such there is no law (Galatians 5:22,23).

These qualities begin to show themselves in a person's life who is filled with the Spirit. The produce a Christlike character in the individual. These attributes include:

Love

Love consists of showing tenderness and kindness to others. Love, however, can also be stern. Jesus drove the moneychangers out from the temple because they were corrupting God's law. He did this to as an act of love.

Joy

Joy can be experienced in tough times as well as good times.

In this you greatly rejoice, though now for a little while, if need be, you have been grieved by various trials (1 Peter 1:6).

Peace

Peace comes during trials not from them. The Bible says the peace that God provides passes human understanding.

And the peace of God, which surpasses all understanding, will guard your hearts and minds through Jesus Christ (Philippians 1:6).

Longsuffering

Longsuffering is patience. The more Christlike we become the more we will be patient with others. The Bible says God is patient with us:

The Lord is not slack concerning His promise, as some count slackness, but is longsuffering toward us, not willing that any should perish but that all should come to repentance (2 Peter 3:9).

Kindness

Kindness and goodness speak of helpful deeds done toward others. We are instructed to show kindness to all:

And be kind to one another, tenderhearted, forgiving one another, just as God in Christ also forgave you (Ephesians 4:32).

Faithfulness

Faithfulness means dependability. The Bible makes it clear that God is dependable.

Through the Lord's mercies we are not consumed, because His compassions fail not. They are new every morning; great is Your faithfulness (Lamentations 3:22,23).

Results

When a person is filled with the Spirit it will lead him into an attitude of worship and thanksgiving toward God.

Speaking to one another in psalms and hymns and spiritual songs, singing and making melody in your heart to the Lord, giving thanks always for all things to God the Father in the name of our Lord Jesus Christ (Ephesians 5:19,20).

Service

The filling of the Holy Spirit will also lead the believer into service.

But you shall receive power when the Holy Spirit has come upon you; and you shall be witnesses to Me in Jerusalem, and in all Judea and Samaria, and to the end of the earth (Acts 1:8).

When the fruit of the Spirit has become evident in the believer's life, the results are worship, thanksgiving and service.

CAN A PERSON IMPEDE THE WORK OF THE HOLY SPIRIT?

Is it possible for a person to impede the work of the Holy Spirit in his life? The Bible answers yes.

And do not grieve the Holy Spirit of God, by whom you were sealed for the day of redemption (Ephesians 4:30).

Do not quench the Spirit (1 Thessalonians 5:19).

Work Halted

The great work that the Holy Spirit desires to do in a person's life can be halted when people refuse to obey God. When God's commandments are disobeyed, the Holy Spirit's work is thwarted. Though some people blame their shortcomings on the devil, the Bible says that he was defeated.

For this purpose the Son of God was manifested, that He might destroy the works of the devil (1 John 3:8).

Consequently the believer need not continue in sin.

Knowing this, that our old man was crucified with Him, that the body of sin might be done away with, that we should no longer be slaves to sin. For he who has died has been freed from sin. Now if we died with Christ, we believe that we shall also live with Him (Romans 6:6-8).

The believer can both quench and grieve the Holy Spirit through disobedience to God. Satan cannot be blamed for this, for he has been defeated by Christ. It is sin that quenches the Spirit.

HOW DOES THE HOLY SPIRIT GUIDE THE BELIEVER?

The Bible teaches that the Holy Spirit guides the believer:

> However, when He, the Spirit of truth, has come, He will guide you into all truth; for He will not speak on His own authority, but whatever He hears He will speak; and He will tell you things to come (John 16:13).

> Now we have received, not the spirit of the world, but the Spirit who is from God, that we might know the things that have been freely given to us by God (1 Corinthians 2:12).

Jesus promised the Holy Spirit would come and guide the believer into all truth. The work of the Holy Spirit illuminates the heart and mind of the believer to the things of Jesus Christ.

Spiritual Blindfold

The Bible reveals to us that Satan has put a spiritual blindfold over the minds of those who do not believe:

> But even if our gospel is veiled, it is veiled to those who are perishing, whose mind the god of this age has blinded, who do not believe, lest the light of the gospel of the glory of Christ, who is the image of God, should shine on them (2 Corinthians 4:3,4).

Once a person trusts Christ, the blindfold is removed and the Holy Spirit begins the work of illuminating the meaning of Scripture to his newly believing mind. This helps him better understand the things of God.

IS THERE A DIFFERENCE BETWEEN THE HOLY SPIRIT BEING 'IN' A PERSON AND BEING 'UPON' A PERSON?

Often people speak about two different relationships of the Holy Spirit to the believer. The Spirit is "in" (Greek word *en*) a person when that person receives Christ, and He comes "upon" (Greek word *epi*) a person when that person receives the baptism with the Holy Spirit. Is this distinction something that the Bible teaches?

The Bible does make a distinction, but not in the same way many people apply it. Once the believer has received the Holy Spirit, there is no need to have a second experience when the Holy Spirit comes upon him. There is no basis for the argument that the Greek words *en* and *epi* signify two different relationships between the Holy Spirit and the believer.

People have made too much of the different Greek words *en* meaning "in" and *epi* meaning "upon." The Holy Spirit is said to have come upon *(epi)* Simeon.

And behold there was a man in Jerusalem whose name was Simeon, and this man was just and devout, waiting for the Consolation of Israel, and the Holy Spirit was upon *(epi)* him (Luke 2:25).

Here was a man living before Pentecost, before anyone had been baptized by the Holy Spirit. We know that nobody was baptized with the Holy Spirit until after Christ had ascended into heaven after His death and resurrection. Before His ascension, Jesus spoke of the baptism with the Holy Spirit as something yet future.

> For John truly baptized with water, but you shall be baptized with the Holy Spirit not many days from now (Acts 1:5).

Yet the Bible says that the Spirit was upon Simeon. Thus the Greek preposition *epi* cannot refer to the baptism with the Holy Spirit in the case of Simeon.

No Physical Form

Furthermore, the Holy Spirit has no corporeal form. Since the Bible does not tell us where or how He indwells us, it seems impossible to make a distinction between the non-material Holy Spirit being "in" someone and "upon" someone. Obviously we cannot take this literally.

Thus, it cannot be biblically justified to make a distinction of two different relationships of the Holy Spirit to the believer based upon the Greek words used.

SHOULD OUR EXPERIENCE WITH THE HOLY SPIRIT BE THE SAME AS JESUS?

When did Jesus receive the Holy Spirit? Should we look to His life as a pattern for our own? Is His experience to be the same as ours?

The Bible tells us that Jesus was indwelt with the Holy Spirit since His birth. Jesus was conceived of the Holy Spirit and lived His entire life as the sinless Son of God through the power of the Holy Spirit. However when He began His public ministry He had an experience with the Holy Spirit that some say should be a pattern for all believers. It occurred when He was baptized.

> And the Holy Spirit descended in bodily form like a dove upon Him, and a voice came from heaven which said, 'You are My beloved Son; in You I am well pleased' (Luke 3:22).

Jesus received the Holy Spirit at birth, yet at His baptism the Holy Spirit descended upon Him. Does this indicate that the anointing He received for His baptism is something that each believer must receive after the initial salvation experience?

No. The Holy Spirit came down upon Jesus for the purpose of designating Him to be the Messiah. The Bible does not say that Jesus received the Holy Spirit at that time or that it came upon His life in any special way at that time. It was for the purpose of identification.

Furthermore, His life cannot serve as an exact pattern for ours. Jesus was the sinless Son of God who was conceived and led throughout His life by the Holy Spirit of God. The rest of us are all born as sinners and need a Savior. We receive the Holy Spirit only when we believe in Jesus as Savior. Thus we cannot pattern our experience exactly after His.

DOES THE HOLY SPIRIT BAPTIZE THE BELIEVER WITH FIRE?

In referring to the coming appearance of Jesus the Messiah, John the Baptist said:

He will baptize you with the Holy Spirit and fire (Matthew 3:11).

Does this mean the Holy Spirit baptizes the believer with fire? Because of this passage, many people pray for the fire of the Holy Spirit. But there are various interpretations of what John meant.

Some see this promise referring to believers. On the Day of Pentecost the Holy Spirit baptized the believers as Jesus had promised. Jesus said,

For John truly baptized with water, but you shall be baptized with the Holy Spirit not many days from now (Acts 1:5).

Several days later Jesus' promise was fulfilled.

Now when the Day of Pentecost had fully come, they were all with one accord in one place . . . Then there appeared to them divided tongues, as of fire, and one sat upon each of them (Acts 2:1,3).

Are the tongues of fire the fulfillment of this prophecy? On the Day of Pentecost the tongues were said to have been like fire. There is no reference, however, to the "fire" of the Holy Spirit.

Another interpretation has this prophecy referring to unbelievers. It is a reference to judgment for their sin. In the Old Testament, fire spoke of purifying the faithful and damnation for the wicked:

> But who can endure the day of His coming? And who can stand when He appears? For He is like the refiner's fire and like fullers' soap. He will sit as a refiner and a purifier of silver; He will purify the sons of Levi, and purge them as gold and silver, that they may offer to the Lord an offering in righteousness (Malachi 3:2,3).

The fire of judgment will be a work of the Holy Spirit upon those who do not believe. Another statement of John the Baptist seems to confirm this:

> He will baptize you with the Holy Spirit and with fire. His winnowing fan is in His hand, and He will thoroughly purge His threshing floor, and gather the wheat into His barn; but the chaff He will burn with unquenchable fire (Luke 3:16,17).

Thus, in the context of John's prediction and the lack of any specific fulfillment of the Holy Spirit's fire upon the believer, it seems to best understand the prediction of fire as a prediction of the judgment.

WHAT DOES IT MEAN TO BE SLAIN IN THE SPIRIT?

There is an act known as being slain in the Spirit. This occurs when a person is supposedly overcome by the power of the Holy Spirit and faints or falls to the ground in physical powerlessness. Is this an experience that believers should expect to have? Do we find examples of this in the Bible? The following passages are usually cited as examples of being slain in the Spirit:

So when I saw it I fell on my face, and I heard a voice of One speaking (Ezekiel 1:28).

Then—when He said to them, 'I am He,'— they drew back and fell to the ground (John 18:6).

Then he fell to the ground, and heard a voice saying to him, 'Saul, Saul, why are you persecuting Me? (Acts 9:4).

And when I saw Him, I fell at His feet as dead (Revelation 1:17).

These instances, however, do not actually teach that the Holy Spirit overcame them, causing them to fall to the ground in worship. Apart from the episode in Gethsemane, where the people fell back, the other instances can be understood as people voluntarily falling down to worship God, not being overcome by the Spirit. In addition, those who fell back in Gethsemane were not believers, but unbelievers sent there to arrest Jesus.

Though people have attempted to find a biblical basis for this phenomenon, none can be found. The Scripture nowhere advocates passing out while being overwhelmed by the Holy Spirit. Quite the contrary, the Bible says that the fruit of the Spirit's power is self-control, not some sort of uncontrolled ecstasy.

But the fruit of the Spirit is . . . self-control (Galatians 5:22,23).

When God's Spirit is truly controlling a person's life there is not a showing off or outward theatrical display. Any act, such as being "slain in the Spirit," is not a work of God's Spirit but a work of the flesh. Whenever someone calls attention to himself, he is not glorifying God. This is not the way the Holy Spirit works, for His ministry is to call attention to Jesus Christ.

HOW DOES A PERSON DISCOVER HIS SPIRITUAL GIFTS?

Everyone has at least one spiritual gift. How can someone discover his spiritual gift or gifts.

The Bible does not give us any formula for finding out what the spiritual gifts might be, yet there are certain things we can do.

Find Out the Gifts Available

First, one must find out what spiritual gifts are available. There are four passages of Scripture that lists the gifts (1 Corinthians 12:8-11,28-30; Romans 12:4-8; Ephesians 4:7-12).

Pray for Guidance

Once the believer recognizes what gifts are available, he should then pray for God to show him his particular gift or gifts. The Bible encourages us to pray for guidance:

Ask and it shall be given to you; seek and you shall find; knock, and it will be opened to you. For everyone who asks receives, and he who seeks finds, and to him who knocks it will be opened (Matthew 7:7,8).

James wrote, "You do not have because you do not ask" (James 4:2).

Step Out in Faith

We should exercise, by faith, the gift or gifts we feel God has given us.

But without faith it is impossible to please Him, for he who comes to God must first believe that He is, and that He is a rewarder of those who diligently seek Him (Hebrews 11:6).

Get Feedback from Others

Once we start exercising our gifts, we should get feedback from others to see if we are edifying the body of Christ.

But the manifestation of the Spirit is given for the profit of all (1 Corinthians 12:7).

In exercising his spiritual gifts, the believer should realize that he has at least one spiritual gift and may have more than one but he does not possess all of them. His gift is essential to the smooth functioning of the body of Christ.

Furthermore, the lack of a certain gift in a believer's life does not relieve him from the responsibility to obey the general commands of God. For example, all of us are told to give (1 Corinthians 16:2) whether or not we have the gift of giving. Every believer is encouraged to show mercy (1 Thessalonians 5:14) though he may not have the gift of mercy. Likewise we are all instructed to evangelize (Acts 1:8) though we all do not possess the gift of an evangelist.

To discover his spiritual gifts the believer should:

1. Find out what gifts are available.

2. Be available to receive.

3. Pray for God's guidance.

4. Step out in faith.

5. Get feedback from others.

IS POSSESSION OF SPIRITUAL GIFTS EQUATED WITH SPIRITUAL MATURITY?

Some people feel that the more gifts one has, the more spiritual he becomes. But the Bible does not equate spiritual gifts with being spiritual.

The Apostle Paul told the Corinthian church that they were second to none in the matter of spiritual gifts:

> You were enriched in everything by Him in all utterance and all knowledge, even as the testimony of Christ was confirmed in you, so that you come short in no gift, eagerly waiting for the revelation of our Lord Jesus Christ (1 Corinthians 1:5-7).

However, this same church, which had many spiritual gifts, was described in the following manner:

> And I brethren, could not speak to you as to spiritual people but as to carnal, as to babes in Christ. . . for you are still carnal. For where there are envy strife, and divisions among you, are you not carnal and behaving like mere men? (1 Corinthians 3:1,3).

This church was ravaged with problems. Therefore, it is not accurate to equate spiritual gifts with spiritual maturity. The gifts of the Spirit are the means. The fruit of the Spirit is the desired goal.

But the fruit of the Spirit is love, joy, peace, longsuffering, kindness, goodness, faithfulness, gentleness, self-control. Against such there is no law (Galatians 5:22,23).

WHY DON'T BELIEVERS TODAY PERFORM THE SAME MIRACULOUS WORKS AS EARLY CHRISTIANS?

The Bible records that the early Christians performed mighty works.

> And through the hands of the apostles many signs and wonders were done among the people. . . So that they brought the sick out into the streets and laid them on beds and couches, that at least the shadow of Peter passing by might fall on some of them. Also a multitude gathered from the surrounding cities to Jerusalem, bringing sick people and those who were tormented by unclean spirits, and they were all healed (Acts 5:12,15,16).

These miracles were not limited to the apostles. Stephen, who was not an apostle, also performed miracles.

> And Stephen, full of faith and power, did great wonders and signs among the people (Acts 6:8).

The New Testament says the miracles caused many to believe in Jesus. The signs that they performed were not denied by the unbelievers. After one particular miracle, the religious leaders concluded:

What shall we do to these men? For, indeed, that a notable miracle has been done through them is evident to all who dwell in Jerusalem, and we cannot deny it (Acts 4:16).

Though there are those who contend that the same miracles are occurring today, they are certainly not happening with the same regularity as in the New Testament period. Moreover it is not the normal experience for any church or believer. Why don't we see the same type of things happening today? Should the believer expect to see these miraculous signs? The following answers are given for the lack of miraculous deeds performed by the church today:

1. The miracles were limited to the apostolic age as a confirmation of the truth of the gospel.

2. Sin and a lack of faith on the part of believers keep miracles from occurring.

3. Miracles are still possible but not the norm.

Limited to the Apostolic Age

Among the reasons for the miracles was to establish the truth of the gospel. There are verses that speak of the confirmation of Christ's message by miracles.

How shall we escape if we neglect so great a salvation, which at first began to be spoke by the Lord, and was confirmed to us by those who heard Him, God also bearing witness both with signs and wonders, with various miracles, and the gifts of the Holy Spirit, according to His own will? (Hebrews 2:3,4).

If the confirmation of the gospel were the only reason for these miracles, then after the word had been confirmed there was no further need for signs. Some people argue that this is why we do not see the miracles performed today: B. B. Warfield gave a classic statement of that position:

Had any miracles perchance occurred beyond the Apostolic age they would be without significance; mere occurrences with no universal meaning. What is important is that the Holy Scriptures teach clearly that the complete revelation of God is given in Christ, and that the Holy Spirit who is poured out on the people of God has come solely in order to glorify Christ and to take the things of Christ. Because Christ is all in all, and all revelation and redemption alike are summed up in him, it would be inconceivable that either revelation or accompanying signs should continue after the completion of that great revelation with its accrediting works (B.B. Warfield, *Counterfeit Miracles*, Banner of Truth Trust, 1918, reprinted 1976, pp. 27,28).

This argument sees the purpose of miracles as limited to confirmation of Christ. If that were the purpose for the miracles, then we should not expect see modern-day miracles. Yet, if this were the purpose of the miraculous gifts, we should expect to see it every time, or at least more often, than it does occur in the New Testament. If that were the case, we should expect to see the miracles on every occasion of the early presentation of the gospel.

Sin and Lack of Faith

There are others who feel the lack of miracles lay not so much with God but with man's spiritual state. People have refused to believe in God for the miracles and that is why they do not occur. Yet, this position also assumes that miracles should be the norm for the New Testament era and the Bible does not portray it that way.

Possible Today But Not the Norm

It seems better to take the position that miraculous signs could have intensified during various periods of the history of the church without dying out altogether. Miracles, on the order of those performed by the apostles, having not been the norm for the church age. There have been reports of some of these miracles occurring on occasion, but their frequency and verifiability has not been the same as with the apostolic times.

While it does not seem right to rule out the possibility of modern-day miracles, we should not expect this to be the norm.

We conclude:

1. The apostles clearly performed miracles, but miracles were not the norm.

2. One reason these signs were performed was for the establishment of the truth of the gospel.

3. Some believe that the confirmation of the gospel was the only reason miracles were performed. Once the message had been confirmed, miracles of that order ceased. However this argument does not fit the facts.

4. Others see the lack of miracles as due to sin and faithlessness in the church.

5. It is better to realize that miracles are not the norm for the church age, yet still can occur on occasion when God sees fit.

SHOULD A PERSON WHO IS SICK SEEK SUPERNATURAL HEALING?

A practical question arises as to what to do when one is sick. Should a person seek God on all occasions for a supernatural healing? Is consulting a doctor a sign of a lack of faith?

Whenever someone is sick, prayer to God is always the proper thing to do.

> Is anyone among you sick? Let him call for the elders of the church and let them pray over him, anointing him with oil in the name of the Lord (James 5:14).

But it does not necessarily mean that the person should leave it at that, for God can heal in a variety of ways: instantly, through natural processes, through medicine, in the resurrection.

Instantly

There are occasions where God will heal someone instantly when that person is prayed for. This is a distinct possibility, but this is not what normally occurs. If someone does not become healed after prayer, he should not feel out of favor with God.

Through Natural Processes

Sometimes the healing will not take place instantly but will occur gradually. God will give the person the grace to endure while is in the process of being healed.

Through Medicine

Sometimes God will have the believer see a doctor and become healed through medicine. This does not show a lack of faith. Human means are permissible when it comes to receiving healings. Moreover, it is not a failure when someone prays to be healed and remains sick.

In the Resurrection

There are occasions when the believer will not be healed in this life. Some will have to suffer until death. Their healing will take place in the resurrection when God restores their body to wholeness.

So when this corruptible has put on incorruption, and this mortal has put on immortality, then shall be brought to pass the saying that is written: Death is swallowed up in victory (1 Corinthians 15:54).

God does heal apart from the gift of healing. When a person is sick, he should seek God for a healing, but this does not mean that other precautions should be ignored, such as visiting a doctor and taking medicine.

It must be understood that God does not have to heal someone to prove He is God. Many times the character of God is put in question as a result of sickness. God must "prove Himself."

But nowhere in Scripture is He committed to doing this. Also it is not necessary to equate healing with believing in the supernatural. One can believe in the supernatural and the healing power of God and still not be healed.

MUST A PERSON SPEAK IN TONGUES TO BE SAVED?

Is it necessary for a person to speak in tongues to be saved? Those who say so usually refer to a statement by the Apostle Paul:

I wish that you all spoke in tongues (1 Corinthians 14:5).

Also cited are examples in the Book of Acts where people exhibited the gift of tongues when they were saved (Acts 10:19). Yet the Bible nowhere equates the gift of tongues with salvation.

The Apostle Paul asked the question, "Do all speak with tongues?" (1 Corinthians 12:30). The way the sentence is structured in the Greek demands that the answer be no. All believers do not speak in tongues.

When the Apostle Paul said to the Corinthians that he wished all of them spoke in tongues, he was not advocating that they do this. The remainder of the verse reads, "but even more that you prophesied" (1 Corinthians 14:5).

Furthermore, tongues are not a sign to the believer but to the unbeliever:

Therefore tongues are for a sign, not to those who believe, but to unbelievers (1 Corinthians 14:22).

With two exceptions, new believers in the Book of Acts did not speak in tongues, there is no record that the three thousand who believed that day spoke in tongues when they believed.

The Bible teaches that salvation is a free gift from God. It is accepted by faith, and no visible sign must accompany it.

For by grace you have been saved through faith, and that not of yourselves; it is the gift of God, not of works, lest anyone should boast (Ephesians 2:8,9).

SHOULD A PERSON SEEK TO SPEAK IN TONGUES?

Should everyone seek the gift of tongues? There are those who encourage every believer to speak in tongues. The Scriptures speak of tongues as a gift from God. But most of the things said about the gift warn against its abuse and emphasize its proper place among spiritual gifts. The Bible does not encourage or command the believer to seek to speak in tongues:

Do all speak with tongues? Do all interpret? But earnestly desire the best gifts (1 Corinthians 12:30,31).

Many people in the Corinthian church practiced the gift of tongues but nevertheless were described by Paul as "carnal" believers. Thus the gift of tongues, like other gifts, is not equated with spirituality.

Tongues are never to serve as a rallying force, as some people contend. Jesus Christ is the one who unites us, not the gifts of the Spirit. Because of its unusual nature the gift of tongues has attracted more interest than it deserves, but as the Bible says the gift should be kept in proper perspective.

Therefore, we conclude about seeking to speak in tongues:

1. Nowhere is the believer encouraged to seek to speak in tongues.

2   Tongue-speaking is not related to spiritual maturity.

3   Speaking in tongues is not to be a rallying force for believers.

4   Tongue-speaking is not a method of spiritual growth.

DOES SPEAKING IN TONGUES HAVE A DEVOTIONAL PURPOSE?

The gift of tongues was given for the purpose of edifying the body of Christ. Is it permissible, then, for the believer to pray by himself to God in tongues?

The Bible says tongues can be a personal edification of the speaker.

> He who speaks in tongues edifies himself, but he who prophesies edifies the church (1 Corinthians 14:4).

This could be what the apostle had in mind when he talked about praying in the Spirit.

> Praying always with all prayer and supplication in the Spirit (Ephesians 6:18).

Only God understands when someone prays in this manner.

> For he who speaks in a tongue does not speak to men, but to God, for no one understands him . . . For if I pray in a tongue, my spirit prays, but my understanding is unfruitful (1 Corinthians 14:2,14).

Sometimes a believer doesn't know how to pray. He perhaps cannot express himself in prayer, and words seem inadequate. He may use the gift of tongues then as a private prayer language between himself and God.

Likewise the Spirit also helps in our weaknesses. For we do not know what we should pray for as we ought, but the Spirit Himself makes intercession for us with groanings which cannot be uttered (Romans 8:26).

Some Christians do not see a devotional purpose for tongues. They argue that 1 Corinthians 14:4 does not deal with the purpose of the gift, but speaks of the by-product of the gift. Therefore, self-edification is not a valid goal. The gifts of the Spirit have been given for the edification of the body, not the individual.

But the manifestation of the Spirit is given to each one for the profit of all (1 Corinthians 12:7).

WHAT DOES IT MEAN TO PRAY IN THE SPIRIT?

The Bible says we are to "pray in the Spirit":

Praying always with all prayer and supplication in the Spirit (Ephesians 6:18).

What does this mean? How does someone pray in the Spirit?

The word translated "in" can mean "in," "with," or "by means of." The above verse refers to our need of the Holy Spirit to help us with our prayers.

Likewise the Spirit also helps us in our weaknesses. For we do not know what we should pray for as we ought, but the Spirit Himself makes intercession for us with groanings that cannot be uttered (Romans 8:26).

Often, we do not know how to pray or what we should pray for. This is why we need the Holy Spirit to help us. The Apostle Paul may have been contrasting praying with the Spirit (tongues) as opposed to praying with the mind.

For if I pray in a tongue, my spirit prays, but my understanding is unfruitful. What is the result then? I will pray with the spirit, and I will also pray with the understanding (1 Corinthians 14:14,15).

We can see in this verse that the Holy Spirit intercedes on our behalf, and brings to mind the things for which we should pray.

IS IT PROPER TO GATHER TO SPEAK IN TONGUES?

Is it proper procedure for believers to assemble for the purpose of speaking in tongues? Do we find an example of this in Scripture? The Bible records tongue-speaking on the following occasions:

The Coming of the Holy Spirit

In the three instances in the Book of Acts where speaking in tongues is recorded, they all have to do with the coming of the Holy Spirit. On the Day of Pentecost, in Samaria, and in Ephesus we find the tongues used in connection with reception of the Holy Spirit. It was a spontaneous happening, not something that was planned.

During Worship Services

The only other biblical example that the Bible gives of tongue-speaking was during the gathering of believers. However, on these occasions the believers assembled for the purpose of instruction, not for speaking in tongues. The Apostle Paul made this clear:

> Yet in the church I would rather speak five words with my understanding, that I my teach others also, than ten thousand words in a tongue (1 Corinthians 14:19).

Thus, the Bible records tongue-speaking on only two different situations, the coming of the Holy Spirit and the worship service. There is no example of believers gathering for the purpose of speaking in tongues.

CONCLUSION TO PART 4

After surveying what the Bible says about the way the Holy Spirit works in the lives of individuals we come to the following conclusions:

1. A person must be born of the Spirit to become a Christian.

2. Everyone who believes in Jesus receives the Holy Spirit.

3. The Holy Spirit is given to guide the believer.

4. The believer cannot lose the Holy Spirit.

5. Tongue-speaking is not necessary for salvation or for leading a spiritual life.

SUMMARY

Our study of the person, work, and ministry of the Holy Spirit has taught us many things. We have discovered that He is more than just a godly influence. He is God, the Third Person of the Trinity. As God, the Holy Spirit has been involved in the functioning of the universe. During the Old Testament period, He provided wisdom and guidance to those who served God.

The Holy Spirit is the one who guided the earthly life of Jesus. On the Day of Pentecost He came down in a unique way to empower believers for service. When Christ ascended to heaven and sent the Holy Spirit down to earth, He gave gifts to believers to build up His kingdom. Spiritual gifts have been an area of division for so many believers. This is tragic. Believers must not have an "us versus them" mentality. It is perfectly acceptable to have a differing point of view on how some of the gifts of the Spirit work. However, it is not acceptable to let these differences cause divisions among the faithful.

Finally, we have seen that the Holy Spirit lives and operates in the life of the believers. He desires to produce the fruit of the Spirit in our lives, to make us more Christlike. This should be the goal for each of us, for nothing in this world is more important.

ABOUT THE AUTHOR

Don Stewart

Don Stewart is one of the most successful writers in the country having authored or co-authored over twenty books. These include *You Be The Judge, The Coming Temple* and *Ten Reasons To Trust the Bible.*

Don's writings have also achieved international success. Twenty-four of his titles have been translated into different languages including Chinese, Finnish, Polish, Spanish, German, and Portuguese.

Don received his undergraduate degree at Biola University majoring in Bible. He received a masters degree from Talbot Theological Seminary graduating with the highest honors. Don is a member of the national honor society, Kappa Tau Epsilon.

Don is also an internationally known apologist, a defender of the historic Christian faith. In his defense of Christianity he has traveled to over thirty countries speaking at colleges, universities, churches, seminars, and retreats. His topics include the evidence for Christianity, the identity of Jesus Christ, the challenge of the cults, and the relationship of the Bible and science.

Because of his international success as an author and speaker, Don's various books have generated sales of over one million copies.

Other Books By Don Stewart
from Dart Press

You Be The Judge: Is Christianity True?

Ten Reasons To Trust The Bible (formerly titled The Ten Wonders Of The Bible).

The Coming Temple (with Chuck Missler)

Basic Bible Study Series

* What Everyone Needs To Know About **God**

* What Everyone Needs To Know About **Jesus**

* What Everyone Needs To Know About **The Bible**

To order books call toll free
1-800-637-5177

Books Coming From Don Stewart
in 1992

In Search of the Lost Ark: The Quest for the Ark of the Covenant

Basic Bible Study Series

* What The Bible Says About **Science**

* What The Bible Says About **The Future**